Package, Position, Profit:
How to Build a Legal Practice the 21st Century Wants to Buy

DOUGLAS McPHERSON

Head of events and books
Leah Darbyshire

Commissioning editor
Laura Slater

Editorial assistant
Edward Bowes

Published by
Globe Law and Business Ltd
3 Mylor Close
Horsell
Woking
Surrey GU21 4DD
United Kingdom
Tel: +44 20 3745 4770
www.globelawandbusiness.com

ISBN: 978-1-78358-282-2
A catalogue record for this book is available from the British Library

Contents

About the author

After graduating in marketing and post-graduating in advertising, Douglas went into sales thinking that if he could sell he'd never be out of work. Although it was meant to be a temporary step – a purely education-finishing assignment – he has never looked back.

His association with the professional services began in 1994 when he joined Intellectual Property Publishing where he soon became sales manager of the IP portfolio, and ultimately sales and marketing manager for the owning group, Armstrong.

When Armstrong was sold to Lloyd's of London Press, Douglas was promoted to commercial director of the Lloyd's Marine Intelligence Unit with full responsibility for promoting, packaging, and selling Lloyd's of London's market-leading shipping data output. This role saw him continue to work closely with the professional services, most notably the international Admiralty Law, marine underwriting, and marine finance and actuarial sectors, across the world's major shipping centres.

In 2009, Douglas joined Bernard Savage at Size 10½ Boots, a Business Development Agency that works solely with the professional services, helping professionals to win more new clients and more work from the clients they already have.

The tips, tricks, and shortcuts in *Package, Position, Profit* and Douglas's first book, *The Visible Lawyer* (ARK Group, 2016), are the result of a combination of Size 10½ Boots' partners' corporate and professional services experience and the no-nonsense, plain speaking, straightforward approach they have developed alongside their constantly growing client list.

Because of the nature of self-employment, there is never a lot of spare time, but any time Douglas does have is spent with family, coaching youth football, collecting obscure soul records, and enjoying a second honeymoon with Chelsea Football Club thanks to the arrival of Antonio Conte.

Executive summary

The legal market refuses to stand still. While the muttering about AI and virtual practices rumbles on, unsettling many of the more traditional firms' views of the future, the level of competition within the industry continues to rise rapidly and apparently unabated.

Law firms today have to compete with new market entrants (a list that includes many instantly recognisable high street names, all backed by large and generously funded marketing machines), in-house legal teams handling more work for their internal clients and increasingly attracting talent from private practice, and other professionals – most notably accountants – who are starting to encroach on some of the practice areas that were once the preserve of the lawyer.

And competition has only been heightened by the unparalleled level of consolidation in the market. There have never been so many mergers and acquisitions within the legal world and the new larger, stronger (in theory at least) entities this activity has created add another threat to the remaining firms in their markets.

Simultaneously, the level of pressure being exerted by clients on firms is at an all-time high. Technology has inflated expectations over response times and accessibility, and recognition of the increased competition between firms for their business has given clients an opportunity to squeeze lawyers on fees and force law firms to offer them more and more in terms of 'value adds'.

But although this may look bleak, is this a bad time to be a law firm? Not at all. As in all walks of life, threats present themselves in step with opportunities. The only thing is, if you are to pilot your firm, practice, or department through the next phase of the legal industry's development, you need to ensure you are as attractive as you can be to the clients you want.

If you are to achieve that, you need to be cannier in the way you take your firm to market; and to do that, you need to be more sophisticated in the way that you package what you have to offer in terms of your credentials, your service offering and service levels, your personnel, and your specialisms.

You need to choose the right market position for your firm. You also need to know that package (or, if relevant, those packages) are priced correctly, in the way that suits your clients best, and in a way that supports the market position you aspire to.

Once you have all of those ingredients, you can start to promote your package and your pricing to the market(s) you have chosen to pursue. However, because you have made real decisions as to what those markets are and have agreed the position you would like to attain in those markets, this is no longer a scattergun activity; it will be a focused and carefully planned campaign which, in turn, should reap higher rewards for lower costs.

The good news is that if you get the packaging, positioning, and promotion right, you are well on the way to winning the work you want at the fee level you want, and that simply has to be the most direct route to profitable growth.

This book has been written to help you do just that: to show you how to package and position your firm in a way that will allow you to profit from your efforts. We'll cut through some of the marketing-speak that all too often either prevents or puts lawyers off getting to the heart of building a viable, relevant marketing strategy. We'll also look at some practical examples of how best to design the right strategy for your firm and, most importantly of all, how you can implement those ideas easily so that they start delivering commercial success.

Chapter 1 provides an introduction to the legal market today, considers the developments that are likely to have an impact on firms of all sizes in the not-too-distant future, and spells out why it will only become more important to package, position, and promote your law firm more commercially, more creatively, and more effectively.

Chapter 2 then explores the first steps towards building a law firm 21st-century clients want to buy. We look at Kotler's four Ps (product, position, price, and promotion), which provide a structure for a successful marketing strategy, and how to apply these to a law firm today, including the kinds of questions you need to be thinking about (and able to answer) as a firm in each of the four key areas.

Chapter 3 challenges you to think about your strengths, weaknesses, and what your clients value most about your firm. This chapter takes you through the process for designing and building a client value proposition (CVP) that really sets out what clients gain from working with your firm, and how to manage that process internally.

Chapter 4 explains how you actually use your client value proposition so that it's embedded in everything you do and is tangible in every 'touchpoint' a client, contact, or target has with your firm. I include examples of how CVPs can be, and have been, used successfully, for example in pitch situations, through website design, or in the language and mediums you use when communicating with clients.

Chapter 5 focuses on positioning your firm. We consider key questions such as what positioning really means in a legal market context, how to choose how and where to position your firm, and what part brand plays within the positioning process.

Chapter 6 shares six stories from legal service providers in the US and UK that have done an exemplary job of packaging and positioning their firms in today's competitive legal market. In each case, I spoke to those closest to the projects these firms had implemented for a full and frank appraisal of exactly what they did and what they have achieved.

Having gone through the process of designing a CVP and packaging your firm in the way that best fits the market position you want, all of that work will be wasted if you come up with a pricing structure that contradicts your message. Chapter 7 tackles how to come up with a strategy that aligns with your offering and the market position you occupy or aspire to.

Finally, in the Epilogue, I ask you to consider the final, essential ingredient by which all of your strategies and processes will stand or fall: your people.

Dedication

As well as the NG2 branch of the Clan McPherson, this book is for Bernard Savage, the other half of Size 10½ Boots to thank him for his friendship, partnership, and support over the last however many years... and in the vain hope he reads it and finally finds out what a client value proposition really is!

Chapter 1:
An introduction to today

Where is the legal market today?

Well that really is the $64-million question, isn't it? Depending on who you talk to, and on which day, the legal industry is either at death's door or about to embark on the trip of a lifetime. To compound matters further, both views are supported by compelling and highly credible arguments, put forward by equally compelling and credible legal figures.

As we are faced with quite a spectrum, let's start with what we know. The legal market is certainly more complex than ever before and the reasons for that include the following:

1. Increased competition

This has to be the starting point because the fact that the legal market has never been this competitive is:

- Something we all need to wholeheartedly agree on before we go any further; and
- The number one threat to every law firm today (whatever your size, wherever you're based, whatever specialism(s) you offer).

I'm no economist but I do recognise that the more competitive a market is, the more options exist for consumers; and the more options that exist, the harder it is for those individual options to stand out. If legal service providers can't stand out from the crowd, retaining clients while still attracting a new clientele to insulate their future is always going to be an uphill struggle.

Just to compound the issue, the more competition there is, the more pressure is placed on both the tangibles (pricing, client care, service offering, recognised niche specialisms) and the intangibles (how valued and how wedded to a particular firm a client feels, how much added value they feel they receive). This pressure will eventually lead to doubt, which in turn could very well lead clients to explore new options if they start to believe those new options are better, cheaper, or more effective.

2. Increased consolidation

More firms than ever are now looking to merge or acquire, and rarely a day goes by without reading reports of a rumoured or completed merger. The stronger players see M&A as a quick fix, a short cut to growth and to inflating their value and increasing their market position. Meanwhile, weaker firms seem to see it as an escape from their current woes, all too often missing the likely downsides – most particularly the loss of independence – that tend to arise once their share of the acquisition fee has been banked. At the same time, there are of course benefits for both sides. Economies of scale, increased cross-selling opportunities, and a larger purse from which to fund the next phase of growth being the obvious ones.

Meanwhile, for those facing the spectre of a newly merged firm in their immediate marketplace, there is quite rightly a reason to worry. The new, larger entity could well be attractive to some of your clients and their ability to shed some internal support costs could allow them to shave their fee levels, which might make them even more attractive.

Moreover, never forget that consolidation is a two-way street. If your practice is commercially focused, there is a higher likelihood than ever before that your clients will merge or be acquired, and that brings with it its own threats; your client's new colleagues could well stick with their chosen or incumbent legal advisers and force the issue that they – and not you – should be retained by NewCo.

3. Cannier clients

I think it's fair to say that in all walks of life we expect more these days. Whenever we make a purchase, go out for something to eat, or stay in a hotel we want to be courted, rewarded, and generally afforded the level of care and attention traditionally reserved for a new born baby.

Those buying professional services are no different to those buying from the retail or hospitality sectors. Your clients know they can go elsewhere (and would be welcomed warmly for making the move). They also know that you are the ones under pressure to provide all of the value-added extras required to support every pound/dollar/euro your clients spend on your advice.

This is a real threat for those firms who either don't recognise that added value and service are now the key drivers in a purchasing decision. It is even more of a threat for those who pay little more than lip service to this side of their offering, steadfastly refusing to award it the respect it demands. Every client will eventually see through the insincerity and superficiality of lip service. And for those still harbouring a belief that 'doing a good job is marketing enough', this could well drive the last nail into their commercial coffin.

4. Heightened price sensitivity

Alongside a greater demand for added extras, clients also know that in many cases they can also use the increased levels of competition in the market (and many firms' increasingly public willingness to compete solely on price) to squeeze fee levels.

Contrary to popular opinion, this is not just a problem faced by smaller firms. I have seen first hand while working with clients on tenders, pitches, and beauty parades larger firms being told that they need to drop fee levels in order to compete. While many can accommodate a slight reduction by moving work around the various levels of fee earners they have at their disposal, this pressure is still eroding revenue and profitability so it has to be considered a threat.

Waters are muddied further by those firms willing to 'buy in' work in the first instance, thinking (in my opinion, mistakenly) that they'll be able to uplift those fee levels once they prove their worth and the relationship is up and running.

I learned very early in my career that the old adage 'you can't negotiate up' is one of the truest ever spoken. Those clients who push hard to drive down prices in the first instance are not only highly unlikely to be loyal, but are also the most likely to go back to the market for a deal should you have the temerity to attempt to put your prices up.

5. Changing consumer behaviours and preferences

Traditionally when you needed legal advice (and depending on whether that advice was for you or your business), you'd either go to the office of your local lawyers or to the office of a lawyer who'd been recommended to you by someone you trusted. However, that was back in the days when you weren't two clicks on your smart phone from anything you wanted to buy – those dank, dark days when you thought buying something actually required knowing, seeing, or talking to someone.

Admittedly, online channels (and even online referrals underpinned by third party feedback) are unlikely to be a huge threat to large, commercially focused firms; they should still be able to thrive on client referrals and reputation. They will, however, be an increasing threat to smaller regional or private-client-focused practices whose clients will go to Google first, and will be willing to trust what they find there.

If they do like what they find, their decision is more likely to be driven by price and availability rather than location. Moreover, the potent cocktail of the right price and instant availability plus positive client feedback is likely to be enough to turn interest into a purchase.

Location is an interesting point in itself. Skype and email have rendered location an irrelevance to clients in a number of practice areas. Both allow lawyers to arrange conferences around even the tightest of schedules and the instant delivery offered by email means paperwork can be delivered not just straight after a meeting but actually during a meeting, if required.

However, some still prefer the intimacy of a meeting so if location is important, then the timing of the meeting could be the clincher. With more and more demands on a client's time during the working week it could be the firm that embraces late opening, weekend opening, or home/office visits that wins out when a couple of options are being considered.

6. New market entrants

I think it's fair to say that the carnage many expected the aftermath of the Legal Services Act 2007 to herald has not arrived. Some high street names have entered the UK market – most notably Co-Op Legal Services – but it's hardly been the widely expected deluge. However, a number of very smartly dressed alternative business structures (ABSs) have come up on the inside rail. 'Virtual' firms like Riverview and gunnercooke continue to increase their profile and, anecdotally at least, are being well received.

Multi-disciplined ABSs, incorporating lawyers, accountants, IP attorneys, insurers, IFAs, and other professionals (including various general business services), are also springing up and, again, anecdotal evidence suggests they are allowing the law firms they grew from to gain footholds in markets they may not otherwise have been able to access.

On the other side of the coin, some legal practitioners have spun out of their firms to found new, smaller, more focused boutiques. They have recognised their clients want more specialist, more cost-effective, and nimbler, more flexible legal service providers, able to deliver all of the above without compromising on quality.

In the UK, barristers, via the arrival of direct access licences, were another potential threat to the legal profession. Perhaps it's due to many chambers marketing inactivity or many barristers' insistence that good work is all the marketing they need, but awareness levels do not seem to have been increased to a point where direct access has established itself as a viable alternative for either businesses or the general public.

7. Franchises, alliances, and consortia

While new market entrants do pose a threat – albeit a slightly different threat than was originally expected – the much vaunted threat of franchises like Quality Solicitors have proved to be something of a damp squib.

The proposition of these franchises was simple: buy in and they'd give you a national presence, a name, a new corporate identity, marketing collateral (including, in many cases, the promise of peak time TV campaigns), and help with admin and compliance. The truth was somewhat different. I could be critical about individual issues and pick holes in a variety of shiny veneers. I could go as far as saying that even the Emperor wouldn't have fallen for this if it was gift wrapped and stamped 'new clothes', but I don't need to; the rate that the member firms are now either reclaiming their independence or disappearing altogether is proof enough.

But the failure of the franchise does not mean the legal profession cannot profit from strength in numbers. Over the last few years a number of very productive legal alliances have grown up and this could well be where the real threat lies for the traditional law firm.

These alliances and consortia take several forms:

- Domestic alliances – Blanket organisations that provide members with the opportunity to buy in to external advice on non-core subjects like business development, financial management, and IT while offering reduced rates on essentials like PI.
- International alliances – These are designed to introduce their members to their peers in other countries, ostensibly to encourage the referral of clients looking to set up or operate in new territories, but it is also the perfect forum to share best practice and pick up innovative new ideas

that can be adopted or adapted for commercial use within the member's market.

- Referral-gathering alliances – For a fee, leads are generated centrally and distributed amongst members based on location and specialisms.

Whatever form the alliance takes, they all have one thing in common: they work. They allow their members to operate, market, and grow more easily; and in my opinion, as more firms realise that this is both a viable and productive option, existing alliances will grow and new alliances will spring up.

For those lawyers who are content to tell themselves that this trend doesn't affect them, I would remind them that as clients become more price sensitive, as formal procurement becomes more prevalent, and as both businesses and individuals become more globally mobile, at least one of these types of groupings will most definitely affect you in the near future.

8. Consumer confusion

While this appears last on the list, it is probably the factor that persuaded me this book needed to be written. How is the average man (or woman) in the street (or boardroom) expected to tell one law firm from another? There are a few answers I would expect you to table immediately:

a. The quality of the firm's technical expertise

It is absolutely true that any law firm stands and falls on the technical expertise of its fee earners. However, how is a lay client, untrained and possibly inexperienced when it comes to legal matters, supposed to recognise real technical expertise? Is it not taken as read or, more worryingly, just another blanket claim all firms make?

b. Your firm's profile

Profile (in the right areas and for the right reasons) is essential for every law firm, and every firm's aspiration must be to be seen as a leader in its chosen market(s). However, the first step in achieving that objective has to be to ensure you are being seen (consistently) within those chosen market(s). If you are visible and recognisable, potential clients will immediately be able to mark you out from all of the other firms in your area or sectors.

c. The profile of your firm's partners

The answer to this is pretty much the same as the previous one. Yes, marketing-wise it's a huge plus if your partners have a strong public profile – particularly if their profile clearly underlines their specialisms, their approach, and what it'd be like to work with them – but they will never *own* that space. There will always be other partners from other firms on your clients' and your prospects' radars.

d. Your firm's directory entries

Directory entries are a great qualifier. Once a prospective client comes across you – whether that's via a referral, an article, a speech, or a chance encounter – they need to establish that what they've heard or what they felt is actually true. Your directory entries will help them do that. However, if you look at the directories objectively, you are listed in and amongst a number of firms with similar skills, who say similar things, and who promote similar praise. Again, with your objective hat on, is this likely to cement your position in your prospect's mind – or confuse them further?

e. Your firm's recognised specialisms

Being known for something specific is undoubtedly the easiest way to sell your firm. When it comes to buying professional services, the purchase decision is largely based upon the mitigation of risk so underlining you have the right experience and a deep understanding of the sector, geography, or client type in question will go a long way towards starting to strip back any associated risk.

The only thing is – whether you are a charity, a manufacturing business, a software developer, or a repatriated high-net-worth individual – you'll find an awful lot of firms promoting that very experience. However, the fact they may have a page on their website or a recent blog on a relevant topic will not necessarily mark them out from the other firms doing exactly the same.

f. Your firm's history

Don't kid yourself. The fact you came into being 250 years ago after a pact between your city's leading legal luminaries doesn't matter a jot to prospective clients. The fact you are still in business, still highly visible in your chosen markets, and still have people saying nice things about you is what is actually important.

g. Your firm's brand

I've left this to the end of the list deliberately. Still, in far too many cases, what a firm (and I include every type of firm, from the Magic Circle or BigLaw to the high street) considers to be its 'brand' is in fact little more than its name and the logo they use to promote that name. I appreciate this statement will be hard for many to swallow, but I stand by it unequivocally.

Some of those firms have even invested heavily in creating strap-lines, manifestos, and sets of values that underpin that logo and, to be honest, in the vast majority of cases this proliferation of slogans and values is aligned perfectly to the brand the firm wants to create. However, it will never have the impact the firm wants because it doesn't permeate every part of the organisation, so it will never resonate across every touchpoint or create true 'brand value' with their clients and within their target markets.

What does that mean in plain English? It means the brand will never generate the volume of business (i.e. fees) it should. But I'm not going to drop this hand-grenade and stand well back. The concept of brand – and more to the point the way you package and position that brand in order to profit financially from it – is what sits behind this book. In the following chapters

I will attempt to redress the balance and help you create and articulate a legal brand that delivers a tangible commercial return.

What is likely to happen to the legal market?

Obviously, none of us have crystal balls so it is impossible to predict exactly where the legal market will go or accurately predict the advancements in technology that will shape the way certain elements of the legal profession progress. However, if the past is a predictor of the future, then I think we can make some informed assumptions as to what is likely to happen:

1. Even more consolidation

This is not going to slow down anytime soon. On the day I'm writing this chapter CMS Cameron McKenna, Olswang, and Nabarro have announced they are planning to merge. That is not the announcement of a regional firm picking up a local sick puppy for their will bank; this is a collection of instantly recognisable heavyweights making a clear statement of intent to the market. This, in one fell swoop, will immediately create (or, by the time you're reading this, will have created) the UK's sixth largest law firm.

Now, if that model is replicated in the world's leading legal centres and the M&A activity that ensues piques the interest of the large London firms who want an instant, established foothold in the regions then – two steps along the line – we could eventually see a legal landscape that closely resembles the accountancy world.

2. Even more use of technology

If you think back just 25 years, the advancements in technology are bordering on scary. In 1992 it took up to 10 minutes of audible electronic whining to establish an email link that was little more than an onscreen facsimile. Meanwhile, client contact details were kept in hard copy in a central filing cabinet (or on a Roladex, if you were particularly cutting edge) and mail merges were a manual secretarial task – and that's before you even go onto websites, CRM systems, and SEO and social media! Fast forward 25 years and you have more channels to market than you can shake a stick at. All of these produce work so all need to be resourced and maintained.

If you find all of that even slightly worrying, today's lawyers also (apparently) face the threat of being replaced by machines. artificial intelligence (AI) may no longer conjure up visions of C3PO on the Skywalkers' farm or Buck Roger's 25th-century butler, but although the vision of automated mannequins bashing out work is as unrealistic as it is naïve, AI cannot be dismissed as a pipe dream. Some very real AI solutions are being trialled by law firms today and these nascent solutions are currently capable of managing the commoditised end of legal work (although my view is that it will be extremely difficult to develop them further than that).

However, the balance of power still sits on the lawyer's side. If legal advice is going to deliver real value, the legal adviser behind it must be able to combine technical legal expertise and an understanding of the relevant law with an assimilation of the facts and particular circumstances so they can work out how best to apply the former to the latter. Moreover, a legal adviser then needs to be able to underpin all of that with the emotional intelligence to recognise how best to manage and support their client until they reach the best possible outcome. Once you put all of that together – at least in my ageing and highly non-technical brain – there will always be far too many variables involved for machines to replace man, other than in improving administration or reducing basic workflow requirements. That said, 25 years ago I would never have thought there would be email and internet, let alone dreamed that I'd have both in my pocket so I could very well be doing the programmers a disservice.

When considering the potential impact of technological advancements, the increasingly sophisticated coding behind tools like smart contracts should be another concern for lawyers. What is the future for the commercial department if contracts only need to be written once and then, from that point on, they can amend, adapt, and renew themselves? Again, I think that at this point it's a good idea punctuated with too many holes for it to really take hold, but at the speed coding and automated decision making is evolving, who could say this is not a gap a highly intuitive coder could bridge in the near future?

3. A greater emphasis on the added value around the advice

We have already touched on the point that clients are becoming cannier in the way they negotiate terms with their lawyers, using increased competition and higher price sensitivity to their benefit. Well, as you know, their demands don't end there. Clients are also looking at the value-added extras around the advice they receive.

These 'value adds' could be anything from a client portal to football tickets, from training and secondments to strategic introductions to potential suppliers or partners. To complicate things further, pretty much every individual or organisation has a slightly different take on exactly where they derive most value from the client-lawyer relationship. This means client partners need to be attuned to their preferences so they can make sure what is required is delivered.

My feeling is, client demands are only going to stiffen. Yes, an increasingly competitive legal market will continue to be one of the key drivers behind this, but the truth is, it is simply a sign of the times. Consumers expect more from every purchase they make and the professional services can no longer afford not to keep up with market expectations. Firms will need to continue to innovate to make sure their offering always stays one step ahead of standard if they are to remain an attractive proposition.

4. A greater reliance on product development

One of the recent trends on the legal market is the provision of 'products'. These take a variety of forms, including retainers, packages of blocks of time, training packages, advice hotlines, audits, health checks, legal consultancy and online repositories of advice, and boilerplate documents. However, the one thing they have in common is they give the client an easy off-the-shelf idea they can recognise the need for (mainly because each is initially designed in response to specific client demands), and one that they recognise offers fixed scope and a fixed outcome for a fixed price.

Although, on the surface, this culture of 'productisation' appears to sit at odds with the traditional professional services model, it is something that has been welcomed by clients of all practice areas and across all major industry types, which means it is highly likely that it will continue to grow in importance and prevalence over the coming years.

5. A more enlightened approach to pricing

I'm not brave enough to come down on one side of the billable hours versus fixed fee debate. I could give a politician's answer and say that fixed fees are more applicable to some situations and practice areas than billable hours, or say that in some instances it is very difficult to look past billable hours, most specifically when there are a multitude of twists and turns a matter could take and it is therefore almost impossible to make an informed quotation on the total cost of coming to a satisfactory resolution for your client. Both are true and both hold water, but the fact of the matter is clients are desperate for greater cost certainty and, in the main, tend to react extremely favourably to fixed fee options.

However, there are other options open to law firms. Again, retainers (caveated so that clients can recognise the additional costs involved should matters progress) are still popular. Alternatively, you could look at risk/reward structures whereby the fee recovered would be significantly higher than a standard fee if the results outstrip expectation. Or there's the good old fashioned percentage deal whereby you get a percentage of the profit when a deal goes through. There are also layered deals where you would initially pitch competitively, but achieve higher fees if specific terms are included and agreed and/or deadlines or price points are beaten.

Again, it comes down to creativity. Clients want more for less and the traditional open-ended approach (at least open-ended in many clients' eyes) no longer cuts it for many. If you are pitching yourself as a modern, commercial, forward-thinking firm, you need to price your services as a modern, commercial, forward-thinking firm.

6. Alliances over franchises

Given my comments in the last section, it will come as no surprise that my view is franchises will soon die off (and not before time), but the looser, more commercially focused alliances will continue to thrive – whether those alliances are international collaborations between likeminded firms, 'association' style entities, or good old fashioned lead generators. There definitely is strength in numbers and the history of business has repeatedly shown that teaming up with complementary collaborators pays dividends. The legal sector is proof this works, not the exception.

7. A greater focus on 'real' marketing

Let me set my stall out here. I'm not going to hide behind the over-simplification that firms still consider marketing to be little more than a few lunches, a golf day, and choosing a colour to tie together their suite of brochures with the furniture and feature wall in their reception. Legal marketing has come on leaps and bounds over the last 20 years and it is almost unrecognisable from what it once was.

Firms are investing in the creation of an identity, of values, and in improving their profile and their market position. Increasingly sophisticated and experienced marketing professionals (more often than not from a non-legal background) are being brought into many firms to create the brand and client experience to support the growth those firms want to achieve.

The only problem is that because of the unending demand for fees, much of the marketing being done could arguably be labelled as tactical rather than strategic. If one were to be even more unkind it could be labelled as business development or even sales support.

What do I mean? I mean an awful lot of the activity is done for what the firm needs today (enquiries, interaction on social media, tender opportunities... leads) rather than to set out what the firm needs to be tomorrow. The activity centres on what can be done to encourage a trickle of quick wins rather than addressing how the firm will need to be packaged, positioned, and perceived in the future in order to attract a new generation of purchases and the type of client it really wants.

Real marketing involves starting with the end in mind and working backwards to establish the message and the tactics required to achieve those objectives. It requires making some painful decisions about what you need to do to deliver what the market wants, not just endlessly re-treading what you have to offer.

After all, if you can't articulate exactly what you are offering, why you are offering it, why it should be attractive to your chosen markets, and why you are the best option for your chosen markets, how can you expect the message to resonate with the clients you want?

Chapter 2:
First steps towards building a law firm 21st-century clients want to buy

Start with the end in mind

However big your firm, however prominent you are within your market(s), whatever you have at your disposal in terms of marketing resources and budget, you have one thing in common with every other law firm in operation today – you will find it impossible to achieve what you want to if you don't know exactly what it is you want to achieve, and what type of firm you want to be.

If you are going to build a firm that 21st-century clients want to buy, you need to know exactly what you want to sell. That means the first step in the marketing process has to be to gather the key stakeholders across the firm and to make some tough choices with regards to the following key points:

1. What sort of firm do you want to be?

When it comes to packaging and positioning your firm, the way you answer this question is absolutely fundamental. The answer you come up with will ultimately be what you'll be working towards in all of your marketing and business development efforts so you have to be totally comfortable and in full agreement. And you will also need to be realistic.

Aspiration should always be applied and should always be applauded. However, while your vision should drive you, it also needs to be achievable. For example, if you are a regional 10-partner practice with a traditional focus on the private client side, would it be wholly realistic for you to aspire to grow into a full-service firm equipped to serve the largest businesses owned and managed within your region? Likewise, if you are a mid-sized commercial firm celebrating your 10th year in business, would it be realistic to start planning your ascent to the Magic Circle by working towards becoming the go-to commercial practice for the FTSE's top 100 PLCs?

When you are going through this exercise, think about the identity you want to convey as much as the legal side. Do you want to be traditional or modern, service led or academic/technical? Do you want to be local, regional, or national? Do you want to be an open, accessible firm driven by the personalities of your lead fee earners or do you want to be a well-kept secret, relied upon and cross-referred by the cognoscenti within your primary target markets?

In order to finalise this part of the process, I would always suggest testing your decisions against genuine client feedback because the firm you want to be has to be the firm your clients want you to be.

For commercial firms this process is fairly simple. You can either run a client service review programme (using experienced independent interviewers or by having a senior colleague from another practice area conduct the interviews) or you could just bring the subject up at the end of the next meeting you have with your key clients.

For private client practices, you can use anonymous or attributed client feedback forms at the end of a matter. The only problem is that these really only tend to draw out very good or very bad feedback so you miss a lot of the extremely useful stuff that lies in the middle. It may be more effective to take a sample of recently closed matters and ask the clients for their permission to participate in a five-minute telephone interview that would cover their experience and their feelings about the type of firm you are, and the type of firm that – in the best of all possible worlds – they'd like to have working for them.

Sometimes the idea of asking for feedback causes nervousness within the legal profession. Let me assure you, it shouldn't. The majority of clients are more than happy to be involved because, at the end of the day, the feedback they provide is going to improve the service they receive (and because most people simply like to be involved). In our experience – and Size 10½ Boots has run independent client service review programmes for law firms of all shapes and sizes for well over a decade – if persuading someone to give feedback is difficult, there tends to be a much more fundamental issue around the client-lawyer relationship to be addressed.

2. What do you want to be known for?

Again, there are two parts to the answer to this question: you need to think about your legal specialisms and the level of service you offer. All too often, at this stage partners start to look for their 'point of differentiation'. Hours are wasted in meeting rooms on- and off-site earnestly gazing at navels in the hope that all of this cosmetic concentration will suddenly hit upon the reason you are different from every other law firm. Let me save you some time, it won't! Instead, harness exactly what it is that makes you good.

On the legal side, it might be a particularly strong corporate team who have a fantastic success record in completing transactions that consistently surpass your clients' expectations; it may be that you have a long list of successful flotations under your belt; it may be that you have an long client list within a particular industry sector or that you are instantly recognisable as the 'go-to firm' for the well-heeled private landowners in your region.

On the service side, you may be known for going the extra mile. It could be that you are always available by phone or email, even over the weekend or on holiday. It might be that you are known for being able to move your resources around at a moment's notice to take on a new matter. It may be that you have made particularly innovative use of technology.

One of our clients was the first UK law firm to accept Bitcoin payments. They aren't one of the big firms and they aren't headquartered in an impressive EC1 tower. They are a two-partner boutique in leafy West London which proves yet again that effective packaging and positioning is not the preserve of the larger firms; it is a mind-set any firm of any size can use to their commercial advantage.

I don't want to drag you too far into the realms of marketing theory, but one book I have had at my side since my student days is *Confessions of an Advertising Man* by David Ogilvy. Ogilvy was the father of modern advertising and, although some of the ideas, language, and points of reference are now a little dated, the majority of points made in the book still hold true today.

When I found myself flicking through the pages yet again recently with my legal marketing hat on, one passage jumped out at me and I think it is directly relevant to what we're talking about here. Ogilvy states that traditionally an advertiser's assumption is that, if he is to sell his goods, he has to convince his audience that his product is superior to that of his competitors. However, he argues that this not the best way to market. It is far more effective to concentrate on creating positive feeling towards your own offering because if a consumer feels certain that your product is good and feels less certain about your competitors' products, the consumer will buy yours.

Ogilvy goes on to say that this approach is particularly effective when you are dealing with parity products (i.e. a product that is just one of a number of similar products that, to the consumer's eye at least, are all pretty much the same). That is the reason I think this passage has particular resonance in a legal context. Although every law firm is most definitely different – whether those differences are in what you offer, in who you have on your team, in the niches you serve, in the way you deliver, price, and package your advice – to the consumer, one law firm is largely the same as the next.

If you are to break away from being 'just another law firm' and create a truly positive impression, you need to concentrate on getting better known for what you are genuinely good at. You then need to get used to saying it loud and clear, and saying it consistently.

If the theory is right (and let's face it, if it works in the massively complex and competitive FMCG market, it's more than likely it'll work in the more defined and delineated legal world), your ability to articulate your strongest and most saleable properties more clearly will create the required level of confidence in your target audience. It is this confidence that will make them better disposed towards you rather than your competitors when the time comes to purchase legal advice.

3. What do you want people to think when they hear your name?
This is a direct extension of the previous step. Once you know your strengths, have a think about the effect you want those strengths to have on your clients, your professional and industry contacts, and your targets.

Dropping back into the best of all possible worlds (and of course speaking very generally), the response you want will obviously be along the lines of 'they're great lawyers, good people, and they look after me really well'. However, the exact formation of that sentence will depend on the nuances of your business, the practice areas involved, the types of clients you serve and want, and it could even vary from department to department (after all, do you really want your private client people and your commercial litigators being lauded for the same set of skills?)

Again, client feedback can be hugely helpful to completing this step. If you were to ask the clients you speak to what they think when they hear your name, it could both cement your thinking and confirm you are on the right lines – or it could highlight areas for improvement. For example, the common response might be something like: 'They're great lawyers and do everything I ask, but I'm always a bit worried about contacting them because it can be hard to get hold of them. I feel a bit like I'm disturbing them until we get into the meat of the call.' If that is the case then you have a big tick for the legal/technical side, but need to do a bit of work on the service side.

Again, aspiration has to play a part here. As has been discussed in the previous chapter, today's legal market is being driven by increased competition and increasingly sophisticated and demanding clients. If you are going to be as successful as you want to be, you need to develop an offering that clearly demonstrates you can provide both legal and service excellence, but that offering needs to hit home outside your offices and will live or die on the emotional response you create when your clients, contacts, and targets hear your name.

4. What do you want to achieve?

Any marketing plan needs cold hard targets. I still see too many plans based upon woolly objectives like 'raise profile', 'create brand awareness', or 'maximise sector presence'. All of these are noble pursuits but they are not commercial objectives.

If your plan is going to work, stiffen your objectives to the point they can be accurately measured. You need to set:

- Revenue targets – Where does the firm and/or where do individual departments want to be at the end of the year fee-wise? There is no substitute for having a number at the top of your list of objectives.
- Client targets – For some reason, law firms' marketing plans always seem to hinge on new client acquisition. What about the clients you already have? Surely they should be your main focus? Identify your top clients (to use a general rule of thumb, this will probably look something like the top 20 per cent of clients who bring in 80 per cent of your fees) and set a target for how much you'd like to grow their annual billings. For those who operate within a transactional practice (i.e. corporate M&A), you could think of your main contacts – those who refer the most work to you – as your 'clients' for the purpose of this exercise.
- Numbers of new clients – To hit those financial targets, how many new clients would you need to bring in?
- Types of new clients – Build a picture of the types of clients you want to bring in. For example, we are working with a

firm in London's West End who are very clear about what they need their business development to do; they have chosen a specific retailer to illustrate exactly what they want and committed to bringing in a client in the same bracket during this year.

- Clearly identified sector focuses – If your plan is to break into the precision manufacturing sector, say you want a client (or two or three clients) from the precision manufacturing sector. If you have seen an influx of Chinese nationals into your region, say you want to become the first choice for the Chinese nationals coming into your area.

5. What message do you need to promote to ensure you achieve what you want to achieve?

This is a very close cousin of the firm you want to be. However, you need to take the answers you've come up with one step further, and the easiest way to do that is to ask yourself a very simple question: 'So what?'

Asking yourself 'so what?' allows you to pick through your DNA and really cement how what you offer and how you want to be perceived should be articulated so that it develops into an attractive external message for your chosen audience.

In sales-speak these are your 'benefits', and unless your marketing message contains these benefits – and articulates them in a way that directly addresses your clients' legal and technical demands – it will never truly hit home and generate the levels of success you want.

Sometimes this message is referred to as a 'unique selling point' (USP) or as your point of differentiation. It isn't either, and if I'm being honest I don't believe that either actually exists in a legal context. Can you really say, hand on heart, that anything you do is completely unique to your firm or anything you offer is completely and utterly different to anything offered by any other law firm?

Instead, the term I would always use when working with law firms is client value proposition (CVP), which literally means telling people exactly how you propose to deliver value to your clients. I'll pause there for now as we will look at how to create a credible and attractive client value proposition in much more detail in the next chapter.

6. What audience does that message need to reach to ensure you achieve what you want to achieve?

This next part shouldn't come as a surprise – once you know the product you want to promote, once you have the message you want to promote, and once you've agreed what you want the reaction to that product and that message to be, you need to get it all in front of the right audience.

Often when I reach this stage with clients, I draw on inspiration from dim and distant memories of my eight-year-old self. I used to like religious education (I've always been a sucker for a good story and the Bible's packed with them) and one of the things that lodged in my memory from those lessons was the parable of Jesus and the sower of seed.

For the uninitiated, this was a story about the titular sower of seed's continual battle with different types of ground. There were stones, there was sand, and there was the fertile soil and the seed suffered (or, in the case of the fertile soil, enjoyed) different fates in each.

Obviously, the connotation was meant to be religious and I'll withhold my opinion on that particular subject, but what I would say is it is also a very accurate parable about marketing and business development. You can have the best ideas, the most innovative packaging, the strongest message, and the most relevant product, but if you don't find the most fertile soil, all of the preparatory work and creativity you have invested will come to nothing.

Choosing your audience is as key as choosing your product and your message. It is also another area that causes law firms great consternation. We are frequently told 'but anyone could be my client' or 'if I make specific selections I'll be cutting potential clients out'. No. Just no. Your choices should revolve around the most likely audience for your product, the groups or sectors who will be most likely to instruct you. You cannot be all things to all men and if you try, your message will be diluted and you will never create the level of relevance needed to pique your audience's interest and to engage them.

Never forget, all of the people you come into contact with will have personal and professional networks around them so making them aware of you, your firm, and your services will create second level, 'one-step removed' referrals as long as your product is received well, considered to be strong, and articulated correctly.

The other thing to bear in mind when it comes to selecting your audience is that marketing is as much about who you *don't* want to work with as who you *do* want to work with. If you know that businesses of certain sizes or individuals in certain post codes continually baulk at your fee estimates, or question your credentials in their particular area and compare you negatively with your competitors, why would you want to waste your time, money, and effort marketing yourselves to them? Similarly, if you can't demonstrate a credible level of directly relevant experience or offer the service levels an ultra-high net worth client demands, why market to them?

Select your audience with discipline and realism and your marketing will immediately become more productive and more cost- and time-efficient.

Why are those answers essential to your progress?

Although I'm not a fan of this term, I don't have an alternative so for want of a better phrase we'll call the combination of answers you reach having gone through this process, your 'shared vision'. Your shared vision is your statement of intent, your common goal, your desired outcome. It also has to be your starting point because only once you have this – on paper and signed off by the partnership – will you be able to start working out how to get there. If you know exactly where you want to get to you will have the skeleton upon which you can create the

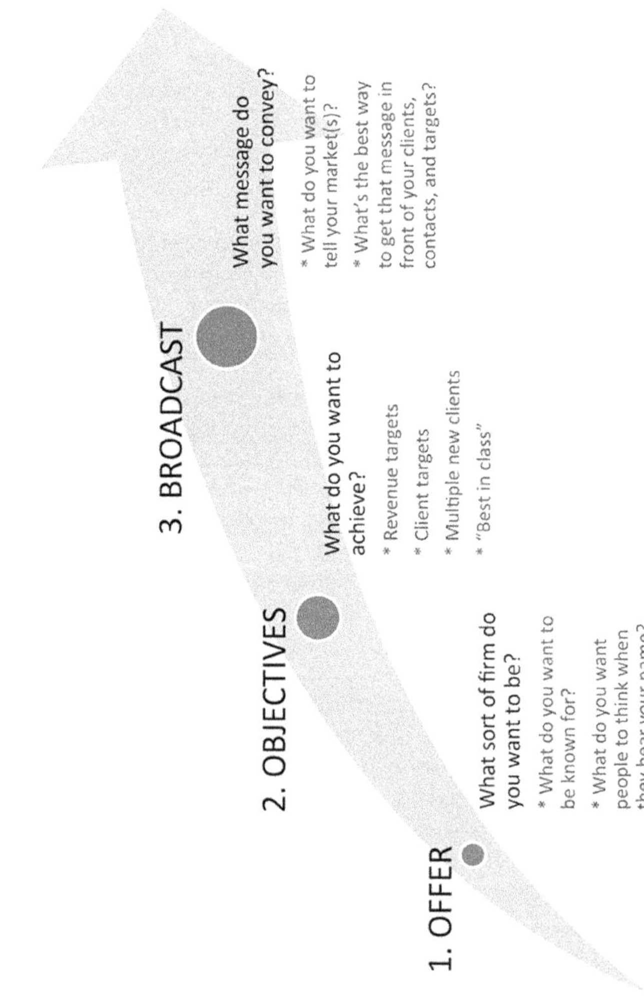

Figure 1: First steps towards building a law firm 21st-century clients want to buy

right strategy to get you there – a chassis you can use to build the firm the clients you really want will be attracted to. Figure 1 is a summary of the process.

ACTION PLAN

Now take five...

List the questions above and jot down some notes as to how you'd answer them. If you're short of time, then stick to these three:

- What sort of firm do you want to be?
- What do you want to be known for?
- What do you want people to think when they hear your name?

If you have a planning/strategy session coming up, it may be worth circulating these questions amongst the partners or colleagues who'll be involved, then using your meeting to discuss them. In my experience, sharing a number of perspectives (after all, you're in the same firm so they should be close!) delivers a stronger result.

The four Ps

On my very first day at university, I was introduced to the 'marketing mix' and more specifically to Dr Philip Kotler's view of the marketing mix. Although this was a concept originally put together in the 1960s, I am yet to find an alternative model that provides such a straightforward blueprint of how to structure a marketing strategy for any product or service.

It also efficiently destroys one of the great myths of marketing (a myth as prevalent within the marketing-related professions as it is within non-marketing professions); namely, that marketing is just about 'getting your name out there'.

Nope, that's advertising (or, to be fair, sales promotion or PR, or a mix of all three) and, as we're about to see, that's just one of the Ps. If you are going to take your firm – and the message and values that underpin your firm's offering – to the market successfully, then it is absolutely essential you give equal credence to all four Ps.

So what are those four Ps?

1. Product

In terms of your product, the types of questions you should be looking to answer include:

- Which practice areas do you cover?
- How do those practice areas overlap and combine to provide a more powerful service for your clients?
- What complementary skills or expertise do you need to offer to complete your offering?
- Where do you need to hire more senior or more junior practitioners to support the quality and profitability of your various practice areas?
- How can you use technology to improve efficiencies around service and delivery?
- What do your clients tell you they need in terms of legal coverage and service?
- What do your clients tell you they *want* in terms of legal coverage and service?
- What results do your services need to deliver for your clients?
- Are there any restrictions or barriers to prevent you from delivering against those requirements?
- Is the current delivery model profitable?
- Are you currently paying to support any features, platforms, or areas your clients neither need nor want?

- What do you want to provide in terms of client experience?
- What will you call your product? (Do you stick with your traditional name? Do you need to shorten/modernise your name? Do you have a specific name for a specific offering or for a variety of specific markets?)

2. Position

In terms of defining your market position, the types of questions you should be looking to answer include:

- How do you want to be perceived?
- Who do you want to be compared to?
- Who do you want as your clients?
- Who do you want as your competitors?
- Which brands/products/services/consumables occupy the market position you aspire to?
- Which level of the market do your targets occupy?
- What type of firm would those individuals/businesses look for?
- What type of firm would those individuals/businesses feel most comfortable with?
- What delivery mechanisms would a client in that bracket expect?
- What additional delivery mechanisms would a client in that bracket react positively to?
- What do the clients in that bracket consider to be standard?
- What do the clients in that bracket consider to be real added value?

3. Promotion

You now have a pretty good idea of what you have and who you want to sell it to, but in terms of how you promote it, the types of questions you should be looking to answer include:

- What message do you want to get across?
- What proposition will your desired clients find attractive and respond to?
- What calls to action will you need to include in order to create a response?
- Where would you expect your desired client groups to come across your name?
- What are the marketing channels your desired client groups respond to?
- Are your desired clients more likely to respond to direct promotion (i.e. social media, press advertising, sponsorship), to thought leadership (editorial, speaking slots, active membership of trade associations, panel participation), or personal introductions from contacts and recognised local or industry figures?
- What part do you expect the internet to play – passive support act or active lead generator?
- What do your competitors do, and which bits do you like?
- Is there any seasonality you need to work towards (i.e. set local events, leading industry conferences, likely spikes in demand)?
- Most importantly, based on past performance, what actually works best for you?

4. Price

By this point you will have agreed your product, the market position you aspire to, and the best way of promoting what you have to the people you want to buy it. If your offering is going to be commercially successful, however, it will need to be priced correctly. Arguably, this is the trickiest piece of the puzzle.

In terms of price, the types of questions you should be looking to answer include:

- What level of pricing is congruent with your product and your (desired) market position?
- What fee levels would the clients you want expect?
- Where are the price sensitivities in your target markets? What are those sensitivities?
- What fee levels would put off the clients you *don't* want?
- How do your fee levels compare with your closest competitors?
- Are your fee levels credible? Do they support the level of added value and service you will promote?
- Do you need to consider discounts for certain groups within your target markets or for the associations or bulk clients that are key to specific parts of your target markets?
- Are your fees set at a level where you could support future growth with minor incremental rises?

Figure 2 (overleaf) summarises the four Ps and the types of questions you should be considering for each.

How do you apply the four Ps to a 21st-century legal practice?

In the most straightforward terms, once you start to break your marketing strategy down into the four Ps your marketing immediately becomes a simpler task, which in turn means that establishing, progressing, or growing your firm amounts to nothing more than:

- Building the right product (i.e. the firm, what it offers, and how it delivers that offering);

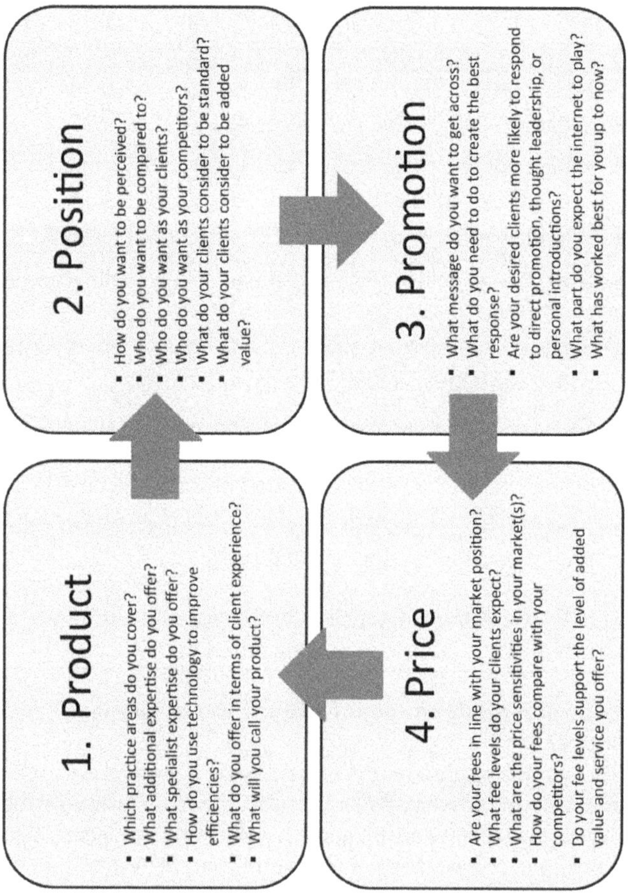

Figure 2: Using the four Ps

- Placing that product at the right level of the legal market;
- Promoting your offering to the right audience(s); and
- Making sure you are priced correctly for your chosen audience.

While (and I hope we agree on this) the model is both simple and logical, there is one potential hurdle to overcome. A lot of hard work – particularly during these early planning stages – needs to be poured into your model to make sure:

- All of the partners understand and buy in to what you want to be and what you want to do;
- You know exactly what your clients want in terms of service and delivery; and
- You know exactly what your market will bear in terms of cost, and exactly how your market defines and recognises value.

You also need to remember that all four Ps need to mesh together and run in tandem because if you get just one element wrong, it could easily bring down the other three, regardless of how well they are planned, implemented, and managed. To make sure that doesn't happen, you should map your objectives (the decisions you made by starting with the end in mind) across the ideas of product, position, promotion, and price. However primitive your final document, it will go a long way to helping you to avoid these types of mistakes.

Now take five...

Take a piece of paper and split it into four quarters. In one quarter, outline your 'product' in terms of coverage, service, and message); in the next, outline the level you'd like to position yourself within; in the next, outline your audience and the best means to reach that audience; and in the last, outline your fee strategy. You now have the skeleton of a marketing strategy, and over the next few chapters we will look to flesh out each part.

Chapter 3:
Defining your proposition

Who are you?

At first look, this may seem like a fairly daft question. Your firm has a name, your firm has a history (the year you came into being; the way you developed into the firm you are today in terms of how many offices you have, which practice areas you service, and how many partners, fee earners, and staff you have), you have an established client base, and you have a marketplace, whether it's defined by geography or sector(s).

And that's a start. However, all of these things are facts (or in marketing parlance 'features'). What we need to decipher and agree upon is *who* you are, not *what* you are.

If you are going to promote yourself effectively, your message needs to resonate with your audience; you need to embody the type of law firm they want or even *need* to work with. That isn't about how many years you've been operating or how many offices or partners you have; it is all about what you stand for as a firm, what your values are, and how you propose to deliver real value to your clients.

When it comes to articulating how you propose to deliver value to your clients, the term you should be working towards is 'client value proposition'.

What is a client value proposition?

There are many definitions available for 'value proposition'. One I think summarises the key aspects of the concept is:

> *'A value proposition is a promise of value to be delivered, communicated, and acknowledged. It is also a belief from the customer about how value will be delivered, experienced*

and acquired. A value proposition can apply to an entire organization, or parts thereof, or customer accounts, or products or services.'[1]

Now let's work backwards and put this into a legal context (not to mention into plain English). As we've already discussed, a lay-client often finds it difficult to tell one law firm from another. They often have a perception that all firms are somewhat expensive, and that the reasons behind the costs may be less than transparent. This is usually because the client or potential client understands the need for your services but not their *value*. This is why the client value proposition is such a vital step for any law firm that is seeking to actively market its services.

Assembled correctly, a CVP will enable you to say not only 'this is what we do' and a little bit of 'this is why we do it', but also (essentially) 'this is why what we do will massively help you and deliver returns far in excess of the costs involved'.

So, picking through all of this, what is a client value proposition? It is:

- A short statement that clearly communicates the benefits that a client will enjoy while working with you, your team, and/or your firm;
- A consistent set of sales messages everyone can use – concise messages a prospective client (or referrer) can easily grasp and remember because they relate to their professional requirements and capture the way they want to be served;
- The promise you make to every client and prospective client as to what extra value you will add every time you work together; and
- An articulation of why a client should choose you as their advisers, rather than one of your competitors.

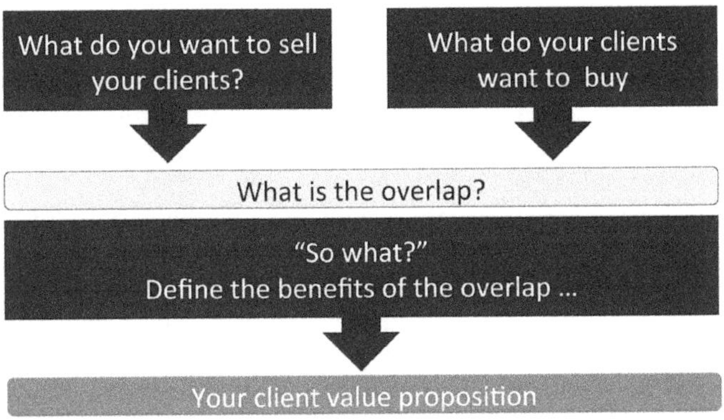

Figure 1: The client value proposition model

What *isn't* a client value proposition?

One of the most irritating developments to affect my professional life in recent years has been the popularisation of the idea of 'differentiation'. To the lucky ones amongst you who haven't come across this modern-day marketing alchemy, the basic premise of differentiation is that every law firm has one point of differentiation – a magic bullet that sets them apart from every other law firm in the world and something that, once promoted, will ensure the firm will immediately be irresistible to the clients they want.

Let's cut to the chase. As I said in the previous chapter, *differentiation simply doesn't exist.* In the average consumer's eyes, every law firm (at least every law firm in the traditional sense) is actually very similar so a client value proposition will never be the result of finding and fleshing out your perceived point of differentiation.

Likewise your CVP is not an 'elevator script', a series of statements that needs to be copied down by all of your fee earners, memorised, and regurgitated verbatim at every opportunity. The elevator script is another disruptive and unhelpful concept that seems to have gained a wholly undeserved level of acceptance over the last decade. Again, its origin is simple. It's supposed to be an introduction you could use if you were to get into an elevator with someone who looks as though they could become a useful contact, with the idea being that it's so short and to the point that even if they get out two floors up they'll know exactly what you're all about.

Although it's simple, this well-honed sales pitch is seriously flawed. The first flaw is that it is completely unnatural. How many of you wouldn't see through the repetition of even the most professionally delivered elevator script? And how would that mechanical delivery leave you feeling? Would you feel flattered that someone had engaged the level of brain power and personal interest it takes to repeat something they have likely used 100 times or more? Or would you feel that the person wasn't able to demonstrate even a fraction of the personal touch that would suggest they have a genuine desire to get to know you as a person and then, once you've established a personal relationship, try to highlight any possible ways you may be able to help each other to your mutual benefit? Yes, I'd go with the latter too.

Similarly, a client value proposition isn't a slogan or strapline. You are looking to find the best – and simplest and most straightforward – way to articulate the value you deliver, not to write a pithy line you can tack onto your promotional material. A strapline could very well be an output of the process, but it shouldn't be an objective at the outset.

And, if you are looking to write a strap line, please remember the line should encapsulate a single promise (i.e. Asda/ Walmart's 'Save money. Live better'). It is not a collection of words that your partners think look good together.

When I'm working with a client to help them define their client value proposition, the way I try to frame it is that it will give them a few hooks everyone can use to answer the perennial question 'so why should I use your firm?', whether they're answering the question:

- In person, i.e. while out networking, when participating in a pitch or beauty parade, when having a beer or a coffee one-on-one with a client, contact, or target;
- In writing, i.e. in a pitch document, in an article for the relevant publications or in the copy you use in brochures, capability statements, and your other marketing collateral; or
- Online, i.e. on your social media profiles and in postings, on your blog, or in the information repositories in your website.

The application of the CVP in most of these circumstances will be fairly obvious, but we'll look at them in more detail in the next chapter ('How do you use your client value proposition?').

The important thing is that, although the core concepts within your CVP must be used consistently, if they are to really hit home with your audience, every member of the team has to articulate them in their own way so that they appear natural – and, more importantly, genuine.

The finishing touch is that they also have to be articulated in the way (i.e. in the language and with the reference points) that is most congruent with the audience they need to resonate with. Law firms don't talk about customers, they talk about clients. Lawyers are professional advisers which means that although abbreviations are totally acceptable (and more so with every passing year), slang probably isn't.

For a banking or corporate group, the tone and language are likely to be businesslike, to the point, and matter of fact, and highly concentrated on commercial success and financial achievement. Meanwhile for a family practice, for example, they will be warmer and more empathetic and focus on the best possible outcome, given what are likely to be extremely emotionally charged circumstances.

Similarly, your CVP is not designed to be copied and pasted straight into every aspect of all of your practice groups' marketing lives. In some instances, the firm will start with a single CVP then rearticulate it for the different practice groups so that it reflects the very different requirements of an employment, commercial property, corporate, or a family client. Sometimes, each group will come up with their own proposition.

If the situation – or the partners or heads of department – demands the latter, then I would suggest there should be a very visible, and arguably substantial, overlap across the finished offerings.

One of the projects I've worked with, in particular, illustrates this point perfectly. It was with a commercial IP practice and the managing partner wanted each of their core practice groups to go through the CVP exercise with me.

At the start of the conversation I was keen to persuade the managing partner that perhaps it would be best to start with an overarching CVP, then nuance it for the different practice areas. He answered my argument with a very simple analogy that has stayed with me since. He told me that the difference in the DNA of a man and the DNA of a chimpanzee was less than 2 per cent, but it is that 2 per cent that both defines and separates the species.

Quite predictably, having gone through all four exercises with the senior people representing each practice group, the managing partner was totally correct; the results were indeed very similar. The discussion and even the wording we used to articulate the findings were somewhat different, but the three core concepts were pretty much the same.

For me, this case study was the perfect way to force me to refine my thinking as to how the different parts of a firm should overlap and interact marketing- and proposition-wise. For the managing partner, it was a wonderful reassurance that he was building a team with common bonds and values – and, surely, that should be the very definition of a 'firm'?

How do you build a credible client value proposition?

There are a variety of starting points. Many firms will already have a set of corporate values made up of core concepts that could be developed to create a credible client value proposition. Similarly, a mission statement will hold some of the main areas that will need to be included. However, although these do provide a great start, corporate values tend to be internally focused and mission statements tend to be a little more lofty; if your CVP is going to work it needs to be focused wholly on your clients and their requirements, and it needs to be punchy and instantly accessible.

Alternatively, if you have done the first 'Take five' exercise in the previous chapter which asked you to take five minutes to write down what sort of firm you want to be; what you want to be known for; and what you want people to think when they hear your name, this too will give you a healthy start.

Or you could take a straw poll across the firm (or at least across the partnership) to find out what those involved think it is that makes you:

- Good at what you do;
- Stand out from your competitors;
- Your clients' first choice;
- Able to provide what your clients want in the way they want it; and
- An asset to your clients, not a cost.

To make the insight that exercise garners even more valuable, ask people to give anecdotal examples to support each of their suggestions.

If all of that looks like hard work (or if, in the first instance, the response is lower than you need), you can also use small focus groups involving the more 'marketing friendly' lawyers within the firm or ask the heads of your various departments/

practice groups to ask their teams the same questions in their meetings before feeding back to the marketing committee or marketing director. However, in my experience, the best way forward is to employ a little bit of everything.

Managing the CVP process internally

If you decide to manage the creation of your client value proposition internally, here is a step-by-step guide to make the process a little easier. (For a summary, see Figure 2 on page 46.)

1. Pull together all of the background information you have

Most of the information you'll need to create your client value proposition already exists. It may be in your values, your mission statement, your pitch and tender documents, or in your brochures, but it will exist. Before you meet, try to bring together all of your promotional material.

2. Pull out the key themes from that material

Once you've got all of that material in front of you, underline/highlight/note down all of the bits you think could/should be included within your proposition.

3. Choose a working group

You may have very strong ideas as to what should be included in your client value proposition, but one thing that I've learned is that two heads are definitely better than one – and five are even better. Having a number of different opinions and perspectives will improve the results you achieve – just don't have too many as you want to keep the discussion moving and manageable. Five is a good number.

In terms of who should be involved and the selection criteria you should employ, my suggestion would be to include:

- Those most engaged in the marketing process;
- Those you feel present the firm most articulately when they're with clients, contacts, or targets; and

- Those who have a strong (but constructive) opinion when they're involved in in-house discussions.

4. Host a facilitated discussion session

The first thing to note about this discussion is that it should be a closed meeting. If you have continual interruptions with phone calls and emails, it won't work (and that includes fiddling with smart phones during the meeting).

The second is to make sure there is a finite slot. If you leave it open ended it will go on and on and, as with the majority of meetings, the laws of diminishing returns will apply – the longer it goes on, the less you'll achieve. The very longest your session should be is two hours.

The objectives of this meeting are to identify and distil the key things you think you offer over and above your technical legal advice: the things you think deliver real value to your clients.

One question I am asked a lot when I help a firm to prepare for this process is how many elements I think there should be. Every firm is different so it's a hard question to answer. The only guidance I can give is if it's less than two you probably don't have enough, and if it's more than four you will definitely have too many.

Remember, your client value proposition should be short, punchy, and to the point; it is not a loquacious manifesto that needs to run to biblical proportions.

5. Don't forget to ask 'so what?'

This is the most important step. Once you have agreed your key themes, take a break, have a cup of tea and a breather, refocus, and sit down again to ask the group 'so what?' This will allow you to identify the benefit of what you are offering.

Again, every benefit is going to be different from firm to firm but, generally speaking, the strength test is that whatever you come up with could begin with 'which means …'.

The second – and again very general – rule is that, when you boil it right down to its constituent elements, the benefit will save your client time, money, or hassle (or preferably a mix of two or three of those.)

For example, if you have a sector specialism, the fact you have that specialism means you will have a wealth of direct client experience and therefore a deep understanding of the issues that affect that area, *which means* you can identify the root cause of the problem quickly (saving the client time and therefore cost); and you can provide the right solution immediately, which will reduce the likelihood that your client will face long, costly, and unnecessary delays to their continued commercial success.

While the 'so what?' test might seem inconsequential; it really isn't. It is absolutely vital. Your proposition could be made up of the strongest, most relevant, and most creative features, but it will not resonate with your audience if you don't spell out the 'which means' (even if the benefit of all of the constituent elements is spellbindingly obvious to you). That is the point where people stop listening to you and start buying into you.

6. Wait a few days, then revisit the notes from your discussion session

Once you have agreed upon your core concepts, and agreed the 'so what' for each, take a break. Leave the results for a day or two (or, at the very least, overnight) and do something completely different. Then come back to them and make sure you are still happy they make sense, are totally relevant to your practice, and reflect who you are and how you want to be perceived.

7. Pull together the key themes

Now you need to summarise the key themes. My preferred formula is to find a very short (preferably one word) heading and then explain it briefly underneath before adding the 'so what?'

Once you have that skeleton, you can refine it so that you have the right heading and one or two short paragraphs of supporting text. (I call that a 'possible articulation' to reinforce the fact it's there to be used, yes, but used in the speaker/writer/networker's own words.)

8. Explain where they've come from

Again this is a personal preference but the more CVP exercises I facilitate, the more preferred it becomes! Alongside the heading and 'possible articulation' I always list out the words and phrases that came out of the facilitated discussion that introduced it. Not only does this give your finished article a bit more credibility when you present it to the working group ('ah, I remember saying that, I'm glad they've taken notice of that'), you also need to remember that when you roll your CVP out to the whole firm, the majority of whom won't have been involved in your discussion group, they need to understand the origins of your ideas and have enough raw material to allow them to express the concepts in their own words.

9. Reconvene your working group and agree the CVP

Once you have your draft headings and the possible articulation, you need to reconvene your group and get their sign off. This will undoubtedly involve a couple of tweaks but there should be no need for major reconstructive surgery as what you present will be a very faithful reproduction of the work you did at the first meeting. You can even cut a corner by emailing the draft to the group and asking them to come armed with their suggested amendments (or to send them to you beforehand) so you can present as close to the finished version as possible, which cuts the time needed for the meeting down even further.

10. Agree the plan and timeline for the staff launch

Now that you have your value proposition, you need to use it. In the next chapter we'll look at different ways of applying your proposition to the different aspects of your marketing and business development, but however you use it, the first stage is to make sure the staff know about it.

1. Pull together all of the background information you already have

2. Pull the key themes from that material

3. Choose a working group

4. Host a facilitated discussion session

5. Go through the 'so what?' test

6. Revisit the notes from your discussion session

7. Pull together the key themes

8. Explain where they've come from

9. Reconvene your working group and agree your CVP

10. Plan the staff launch

LAUNCH!

Figure 2: Creating a client value proposition timeline

Plan a public launch and be prepared to explain your CVP: what it is, where it's come from, why you've gone through the exercise, how it will be used, and the part each member of staff will be expected to play in its delivery and promotion. You may also want to send around an email refresher, add it to your intranet, or use it as a screen saver. I've even seen some of our clients print it onto a card and make sure everyone in the firm has a copy to hand; or make banners, collages, or artwork based on the pillars of their CVP they could display in their reception, meeting rooms, and communal areas.

And always remember, embedding your CVP into the fabric of your firm will not be a one-off exercise. You will need to repeat it in different forms and through the various departmental and team meetings until it takes root.

Once you've decided how you are going to launch your proposition, you need to add the when. Agree dates, write them down (so you have a clear route map you can tick off as you go), and commit to them.

10½. Execute your plan!

Even if the results you reach are a perfect articulation of what you offer and why it will benefit your chosen markets, it will do nothing for you if you don't use it. In the next chapter, we'll look at how best to use your client value proposition and where you should put it to work for you.

Insource the expertise to run the exercise for you

While I have absolutely no doubt that you and your colleagues know your firm – its strengths, its weaknesses, and what your clients value most – inside out, I also know just how fundamental the creation of a strong, credible client value proposition is to every aspect of the process of packaging, positioning, and promoting your firm; it really is absolutely central to every aspect of your marketing.

This means you need to get it right – particularly as, by definition, it's not something you can refresh and relaunch in different words and with different ideas every year. A lack of continuity will ensure your proposition simply won't take root, however strong and relevant the messages behind it may be.

With that in mind, if you are serious about completing the exercise, it may be best to find a marketing professional who understands both the legal profession and the theory behind the client value proposition. Not only will they be able to lead the facilitated discussion stage towards the required end, they'll also make it quicker (not least in the preparation of the draft following the meeting) which, given the billing pressure you're under, has to be a positive.

Someone with wider experience of creating client value propositions for legal firms will also bring with them a wider perspective. They will be able to tell you which of your ideas are strongest and which are all too common in a legal context. While I stand by the fact this will never help you achieve true differentiation, it will help you mark yourselves out from the majority of your competitors and build a proposition that truly reflects where you are strongest.

Once that common ground has been established, an experienced external facilitator should also be able to help you dig right down into the ideas that are left and really extract the benefits that you'll need to turn the features you've identified into a powerful set of statements that will pass the 'so what?' step and really encapsulate:

- What your clients want from you;
- How they want that delivered; and
- The additional value they will enjoy when working with you.

And a postscript...

During the course of writing this book I spoke to a number of partners and senior marketing professionals at UK and US-based law firms about the way they package, position, and promote their firms. One of the interviews was with Angela Hickey, Executive Director at Levenfeld Pearlstein in Chicago.

I will come back to the conversation we had regarding the way she has helped to position the firm for the modern market in a later chapter, but I thought the following postscript would be an interesting way to end this discussion on client value propositions.

When we got to talking about the Levenfeld Pearlstein CVP, Angela explained that Chicago was not just a highly populated and competitive legal market, but it was also a town where everyone knows everyone. Together, those two facts meant it was imperative to create a firm that would encourage the creation of referrals. And for that, it was essential that clients received a service that would make them want to recommend the firm.

'What won't distinguish us is saying "we're very good lawyers"', she told me. 'It's the experience that is the must have.' Levenfeld Pearlstein don't shy away from this position in any way online and if you go to their 'meet LP' page you will be greeted by a banner – in bold and in red – that tells you with absolute clarity that 'doing good legal work isn't what we aspire to – it's where we begin'.

The page then goes on to underline that quality legal work, responsiveness, efficiency, and reasonable fees are just the basics every law firm should, by definition, provide for its clients. Instead, success is about forging a real understanding of their clients and their working and personal lives, and using that understanding to found and fuel effective relationships.

At the same time, the firm doesn't want their clients to experience any 'bitter big firm aftertaste'. This was a phrase that had particular resonance with me, having heard first hand during too many client service interviews how many large firms can be seen as taking their clients for granted, particularly when it comes to service and over-administration.

Angela told me that many of the firm's lawyers had first-hand experience of this too. 'Most of our lawyers came from big firms. As a result they knew what we didn't want and they knew what clients didn't want. We knew that what we needed to do was deliver an exceptional experience for our clients.'

As I've said, we'll come back to how Angela worked tirelessly for over a decade to reach the point where LP have realised their vision of delivering an exceptional client experience, but the point I think that this postscript shows is that if you are going to build a client value proposition that works, you must stay away from the basics and from the beige, anodyne, benefit-free soundbites that have punctuated the legal profession for far too long. When it comes to building a client value proposition that works, you need to step into your clients' shoes, be bold, and be honest.

Reference

1. https://en.wikipedia.org/wiki/Value_proposition.

Chapter 4: How to use your client value proposition

The first rule is: once you've gone to the trouble of creating a client value proposition, you need to use it. I appreciate that this must sound blindingly obvious, but it never fails to amaze me just how many firms go through this exercise (usually paying for the privilege, I would add) and then just tuck the results away two layers deep on their website, or use it once in a new brochure then forget it's there.

The second rule is: you don't just use it, you make sure it's embedded in everything you do. It needs to be tangible in every 'touchpoint' a client, contact, or target has with your firm. When it comes to successfully implementing or – without being too dramatic – *living* a client value proposition, consistency is the key.

All of your staff need to understand not only what your CVP is, but also why it is and where it came from. As we've said, if that's going to work that particular exercise should involve a showcase launch (involving all staff at all levels, not just fee earners) followed by constant reaffirmation until it really takes root.

Once it's out there, you need to make sure your CVP is visible in everything you do. This chapter looks at three main ways clients and prospects experience a firm – in person, in writing, and online – and provides some tips from my own client experience that may help guide you as to how best to use your client value proposition.

1. In person

The obvious application here is when you're out networking or meeting up with a contact or target, or progressing an enquiry.

They will, at some stage and in some way, ask you why they should instruct you and your CVP gives you the perfect answer (articulated in your own way and in your own language, as I said in the previous chapter).

However, here are three more opportunities to promote your core messages (explicitly or subliminally) through personal contact: at reception, through your fee earners, and during pitches.

Reception

Client experience (or CX as it is now often referred to) is one of those buzzwords that has been doing the rounds for a while, and some firms now have dedicated teams responsible for continually enhancing the experience they offer their clients. The frontline of your client experience is your reception. It is often the first impression a visitor will have of your firm, and it could well be the lasting impression they walk away with, so it is essential your reception staff actively adhere to your CVP.

If you are marketing yourself as being efficient and focused on making your clients' lives as easy as possible, then make sure your reception has a record of the visitor's arrival, why they're there, and who they need to see. You will not appear efficient if the visitor is asked 20 questions and then subjected to the ignominy of listening to a call to the fee earner in question to verify what the visitor has just told your receptionist.

If you are marketing yourself as collegiate, friendly, and inclusive, it's probably better if your receptionist is informal, and not hidden behind a desk that would be more at home in a Dickensian dental surgery. Hopefully, they are also not prone to looking over their glasses to ask you haughtily if you have an appointment (I always amuse myself by replying 'no, I thought I'd drive x miles just on the off-chance', when faced with that particular pearl).

If you are marketing yourself as a modern firm with an up-to-the-minute outlook make sure your furniture, brochureware, and PR clippings book reflects this. Better still, offer modern accoutrements like iPads – or at the very least access to a speedy Wi-Fi connection – for visitors to use while they're onsite.

Fee earners

When it comes to meeting your fee earners, do they present themselves in a way that matches your claims? Do they dress in a way that reflects your proposition and the preferences of the clients you want?

One of the firms we have done a lot of work with is a leading media and entertainment firm in London's West End. They dress down every day and while they are all recognised experts in their particular fields of law, the senior fee earners talk in a way that is most 'unlawyerish', but absolutely correct for the musicians, actors, sportspeople, and brand-savvy entrepreneurs who make up their client base.

On the other hand, if I am going to visit one of the traditional commercial practices in the City of London or in Manhattan's financial district, I'm likely to feel slightly ill at ease if the person I'm seeing isn't dressed in a sober-coloured suit matched with suitably conservative foot- and neck-wear.

And please take my word for it, wearing a suit and dress shirt without a tie is not a move towards informality; all it will do is underline your discomfort with the world of informality, so you would be better off keeping the tie on!

Once they look right, it's essential they say the right things in the right way. Do your fee earners speak in a way that reflects your proposition and matches the way your clients and targets speak? Are they up to date with the latest news in your market(s)? Can they speak credibly about what is likely to happen in those markets?

Pitches

Pitches are a perfect vehicle for really reinforcing your value proposition and there is a range of ways off you can – subtly and overtly – illustrate the core elements of your CVP during a pitch situation. The first thing to convey is that you know the business in question's industry, the issues they face, and the issues they are likely to face in the future. A lot of this information you'll have to hand because the very fact that you have been able to respond to the call for tender in a way that has persuaded them to call you in for the beauty parade means you have recognised the relevant trends and reference points – all of which have undoubtedly come from personal client experience.

You also need to demonstrate you understand their 'pain' (what annoys them, what delays their commercial or personal progress, what traditionally have been the barriers to success in their region or industry) and, more specifically, how you would alleviate that pain.

Of course, much of that will be demonstrated in words in your tender document, but the fact you are there in person allows you to demonstrate how passionate and enthusiastic you are about resolving the issues at hand and providing the support required to minimise the effects of those issues long into the future. You'll also be able to demonstrate in person that you have enough sector knowledge to bat away any sticky questions relating to the prospect's pain right then and there (and, again, by using the right language and points of reference).

However, I have also seen even more assured examples where the entire structure of the pitch has been completely built around that law firm's CVP, with the presenters actually kicking off the presentation with something along the lines of:

> *'You saw our relevant expertise and our client experience in our response to your call for tender so we want to use this opportunity to concentrate more on what it's like to work with us rather than go through all of that again. We think the advantages of working with us boil down to (x) key things .... [insert your CVP here] ....'*

From there, the presentation goes on to explain the different parts of the CVP but more importantly, why each component will benefit and deliver increased value to the client (albeit via the adjudicating panel).

Moreover, it allows the team presenting to physically and linguistically demonstrate the different components of their firm's proposition in the way they look, talk, and present in the ways we've already discussed. This is absolutely essential and if you can increase the engagement your beauty parade creates with the prospective client, your success/conversion rates will increase exponentially.

There is a myth in the professional services that beauty parades exist solely for you to regurgitate the complete content of your response to the call for tender in person. They don't. They exist to allow you to show that you are the best people for the job, that there is a personal connection and common style that will provide the 'click' that will make working together as easy and enjoyable as possible. Hooking your presentation around your CVP will allow you to do that.

ACTION PLAN

Now take five...

Thinking about the way you present yourself in person, are you confident you:

- Understand each part of your CVP and can articulate it convincingly in your own words whenever the situation arises, whatever that situation may be?
- Are using the right language, tone, and reference points to support the different parts of your client value proposition?
- Have at least one client anecdote (preferably from your own personal experience) you can recall to support each part of your client value proposition in a face-to-face situation?

- Have got a structure that covers all of the individual elements of your CVP, and that you're comfortable to use in both formal and informal pitch situations?

If the answer to each of these is yes, it's time to put it to the test. If any of the answers are 'no', take another five minutes and jot down some possible answers to use in an 'in person' situation.

2. In writing

We've already touched upon the subject of language (i.e. your writing style needs to reflect the personality you're promoting, so if you're promoting yourself as straightforward and down to earth that is the style you will need to employ). However, just as important as your language and your style is the outcome your content provokes and the service it provides.

If you are promoting a commercial perspective, then your content has to be angled towards delivering clear, usable advice and direction specifically designed to improve your readers' commercial or personal position.

If you are promoting yourself as a practice that is dedicated to making your clients' lives easier, that is the angle your content has to take. Are you sending out content that is blatantly designed to make your clients' lives easier: pragmatic advice they can easily read, understand, and act upon?

If you are promoting a deep sector understanding – for example, in the manufacturing, charity, or technology worlds – then you have to write specifically from that point of view and for that audience. Your written content will simply not be credible if it is written from a legal perspective rather than an industry or sector perspective, or if it's missing the right terms, insight, or topical references.

More than anything, though, you need a 'platform', a defined point of view that you are willing to share. There is too much information available to us all, on every possible subject area, so once you get your tone and perspective right, make sure you are actually saying something. The way you present your point of view will again depend on the personality that underpins your proposition, but that point of view is an essential ingredient; otherwise you won't build the readership you want, which means the time you invest in the creation of your content will, quite frankly, be wasted.

These rules aren't limited to the content you are producing for your own communication vehicles. They are equally applicable to any content you provide for the local or relevant trade press or for online magazines and forums. You need to counterbalance the language, perspectives, and points of view you want to convey to support your proposition with what the audience in question will expect and respond to. On first reading, this might look like a tricky task, but if you know and understand your audience and have created a CVP that attends to their needs, wants, and requirements, you will be well on your way (the editor you work with should be able to add the minor tweaks required to close the circle).

Another point to consider when it comes to written content is the format you use to deliver it – this also needs to reflect your CVP. If you are trying to position yourself as a cutting-edge, modern practice then you probably won't use a hard copy newsletter or even, arguably, 2D email platforms like MailChimp. You will need to have an interactive, continually updated blog, perhaps punctuated with relevant links to recognised information sources and with video content that will breathe some much-needed life and personality into your point of view.

However, if you are providing a more traditional private client experience to a more traditional audience, hard copy is without doubt the best means of directing content. You just need to make sure the 'feel' is right, i.e. the design is in keeping with your audience's preferences and the paper weight and print finish is congruent with the price point, and with the level of affluence of your client base.

Now take five...

Thinking about your written content:

- What language, tone, and reference points should you incorporate into your written content so that it echoes your client value proposition?
- What format and frequency would best reflect the different elements of your client value proposition?
- What are your firm's, teams', and your own personal 'platforms'? What points of view do you want to get across in your content?

3. Online

Although I am still very much of the opinion – or, perhaps, vintage – that puts personal contact straight to the top of the list when it comes to successful business development (although there are of course some exceptions, residential property and personal injury being the obvious ones), the growing influence of the internet cannot be ignored.

Your website is the world's window to your firm. It is where people will go to qualify what they've heard about you; it'll be where people go to find out more having been referred to you. If you are promoting your key strengths (whether they are technical, sector-based, or service-related) in a search-engine friendly way, then your site will become an invaluable lead generation tool – but leads will only be generated if people like and relate to what they see once they arrive at your site.

When it comes to presenting your value proposition via your online presence I tend to break the job down into three elements: design, content, and purpose.

Design

Many firms choose a design they like for no reason other than they like it. This is a dangerous strategy. The design of your website should reflect your client value proposition and make it obvious to every visitor that they've come to the right place when they arrive at your site.

You should be confident enough in your proposition (and, more to the point, the adjectives that support it) to give it to your designer and say 'that is what I want the design to say'. I'll be honest, I'm about as far away from being a designer as I am from being a management accountant (and that's a heck of a long way), but these guys are trained to do this stuff and the results I've seen where the proposition has played a key part in a creative brief have been far superior to those where it hasn't featured.

Now, that's not to say that your firm's livery needs to be lost. Your corporate colours and your preferred fonts can all be up front and centre; what I'm talking about is the visual framework in which they're employed and the images your designer uses to bring your proposition to life.

Content

Again, as with your blogs, articles, updates, and special reports, language and tone are the obvious ways to apply your proposition to the content of your website. The way you write needs to be totally congruent with the elements of your proposition – and always remember you will almost always be writing for a lay-audience so make sure that if you are using legal terms, you are explaining those terms in a way that will be understood by someone who has either had little or no exposure at all to the law.

People want to know they can communicate with their lawyers effectively; and that they are about to receive the advice they need in the way they want it, and in a way that will allow them to take full and immediate advantage of it. If the first experience they have is lengthy and impenetrable web copy, the likelihood is they'll soon be looking for an alternative.

The second part of the content piece is, what content do you actually want to post? And how will that content reflect your proposition.

First off, we are taking it as read that you will need an 'about us' style page, pages for your practice areas, and profiles for your fee earners. You'll also need things like a 'contact us' mechanism and all of the required legal disclaimers. However, from there you can start to layer your pages so that they match your proposition.

If you are promoting a sector focus, then make sure you not only have a page saying what you do and what you've done for that sector, also have a range of content (articles, downloads, fact sheets, 'how to' guides) that mark out your approach for and your credentials in each sector.

If you are promoting yourself as a firm that is dedicated to the local community, make mention (with pictures and links) of the local events you support and the initiatives you are running to benefit your commitments.

If you are promoting a practical approach, make sure you are framing your online content as 'this is what you need to do' rather than 'this is what we can do', and present it as bite-sized chunks people can not only instantly access and understand but also download, print off, and stick on the wall to use long into the future.

Better still, make it easy to forward and share material, so that the readers can become yet another marketing arm for your firm when they send it on to their contacts, friends, and families.

And whatever direction you end up taking, the one thing you must include within your content is your clients' words. Whether you present these as testimonials or case studies (or preferably both), your clients' words will support everything you are saying about yourself and reinforce everything you want to put forward to make your firm more attractive. They will also bring your claims to life and make them a little more three dimensional than flat copy will ever be able to.

Most importantly, because they will relate to people in similar positions, similar roles, and similar circumstances, your clients' words will have more effect on you prospects than flat copy will ever have, and it is that effect that will lead your visitors to actually make contact.

Purpose

When it comes to the purpose of your website, my view is we've moved a long way past the days of 'do you want an online brochure or a lead generator?' Today, every website needs to do both but there are variations and the definition of those variations should be informed by your client value proposition.

Admittedly, many of these decisions will be influenced by the choice you've made regarding the type of content you'd like the website to display – most specifically around the articles, blogs, downloads, special reports, and white papers side of the content. Knowing both what you want to offer via your website and the language, tone, and angle your content should convey will provide the answers to the first two questions you should be asking yourself; namely, why should people come to the site, and what should people get from coming to the site?

However, if your website is to truly underline the different parts of your client value proposition it needs to do more, functionality-wise; and if you are going to the time and expense of creating more and better content, your functionality also needs to contribute to demonstrating the value of working with you.

If you want to promote yourselves as totally accessible and responsive, then the purpose of your site should be to encourage people to challenge your claim. Why not experiment with a heavier and more instant social media presence that will allow your current and prospective clients to maintain contact, ask questions, and receive a 'live' response? Why not build in a 'chat' function whereby, during office hours at least, there is someone on the other end of the speech box ready to respond with a bit of guidance.

And it's important to say that this functionality isn't just a new client acquisition tool. It should also be offered to your existing clients to improve the level of service and speed of response they enjoy.

If you are promoting yourself as proactive and dedicated to keeping your clients totally up to date, you need to design the functionality to 'push' your content out to the relevant parties. That would involve the inclusion of an easy-to-complete sign-up mechanism and the contact segregation processes required to ensure people are only getting updates that are a) relevant and b) useful.

And coming back to the idea of being a modern firm ready to use technology to make your clients' lives easier, think about how you can incorporate the latest technology, e.g. video content, apps like Periscope, and interactive video conferencing that will allow clients and targets from all over the world to join you and receive information, guidance, and updates without even having to leave their desk. The watch-out here is that if all of this is going to work as well as it can and needs to, you need to continually update your delivery and make sure it is being promoted to the right people at the right frequency (and that all of the infrastructure behind the technology works).

ACTION PLAN

Now take five...

Thinking about your online offering, take five minutes to jot down:

- The additional types of content formats you could add to underline your value proposition.
- The changes you could make to the language and tone you employ to create greater engagement with the visitors to your site.
- Any additional tools and technology you could add to your site to make it more attractive, more useful, and more valuable to your visitors.
- The additional ways you could use to ensure you generate enquiries and begin new conversations.

Chapter 5:
How to position your firm

From a legal market perspective, what does positioning *really* mean?

A definition of positioning I like to use comes from our old and previously quoted friend, David Ogilvy. In his customarily direct way, he simply said that market position is: '*What a product does and who it is for.*' The answers to these two questions will give you everything you need to come up with an effective position for your services within the legal market.

If you've been following the processes set out in the previous chapters, you'll already have the answers you need to progress to the positioning stage. You should know what your product is (i.e. what you have, what you offer) and who it is for (i.e. who should want to buy it, why they'll want to buy it, and the value your clients will enjoy as a result of buying your services).

Now you need to decide what level within the legal market you will need to occupy in order to ensure all of those things are joined up and 'what you have' reaches 'who it is for'.

Get this right and your prospective clients will be able to physically see and react to your message and, more importantly, they will be able to recognise your personality and approach is directly suited to them.

How do you choose how and where to position your firm?

In the broadest possible terms, there are three positioning options open to a law firm: location, specialism, and price point.

Location

Are you looking to attain an international, national, or local position? Do you have one office or a network of offices covering your region, your chosen sector, or your primary practice areas' key geographic markets? Is your location key or coincidental to your primary target groups?

Specialism

Are you looking to carve out a market-leading position within a specific industry sector or within a particular legal practice area? Are you looking to cement your position as a credible alternative or a 'first substitute' to recognised market leaders within a particular specialism?

Price point

Are you looking to join the premium-priced end of your chosen markets? Are you looking to be instantly affordable? Or are you looking to be known as a firm that charges a reasonable rate, but delivers a particular line in added value alongside that more medium-to-high price point?

As with all of the areas we've covered in terms of determining your product, personality, and proposition in the previous chapters, you need to be totally honest in the way you answer these questions. I would also suggest that you look at a two-step process whereby you first consider the position you occupy today and then where you'd like to be positioned in three-to-five years.

In many cases, the answer could well be the same. For example, a large regional general practice in Humberside may see strengthening that position, and perhaps encroaching on its competitors' market share, as the best way to deliver the growth it wants. Similarly, for a firm internationally recognised as a leading shipping and insurance expert, cementing that position could see them realise all of their ambitions regarding location, specialism, and price point.

However, for many firms, the focus on specialisms may sharpen. Local industry may have changed dramatically (e.g. the east end of the City of London, which over the last 20 years has moved from low-level trading and warehousing to a hotbed of media, tech, and design) and firms will need to refine their specialisms to accommodate their traditional markets' changing demands.

You may want to expand your geography so that instead of just being known as a leading Newcastle firm, you take a position whereby you are known as the market leader across the North East of England. Or you may want to evolve your position in a specific sector or region so that you muscle into your competitors' client bases and, at the same time, create a level of credibility that will allow you to increase the price point at which you sell your services.

I cannot stress how essential it is to know exactly which position you would like to occupy or whereabouts in the positioning lifecycle you sit (i.e. are you breaking into, sustaining, or growing your position). A precise understanding of the answers to both these questions will help you choose the right tactics, avoid making costly mistakes, and allow you to maintain the level of focus required to achieve and defend the market position you want.

ACTION PLAN

Now take five...

Work out the position you currently occupy in your chosen markets in relation to your:

- Location;
- Specialism; and
- Price point.

And then work out the position you would like to occupy in three years' time. How similar are your two answers?

Please note this exercise works as well for a department or a personal practice as it does for a firm.

The five-tier model

When it comes to segregating the legal market, there are of course many models to follow. The one I tend to lean towards – if only to illustrate the various levels more clearly under some snappy names – is the one produced by Nick Jarrett-Kerr, a specialist in advising law firms on leadership, management, and strategy.

Mr Jarrett-Kerr has split his model into five tiers:

Tier 1: Market Leaders

These are larger firms with dominant market positions, instantly recognisable for their work in certain areas, and able to throw the required resources at any job at very little notice. Their size and budget also allows them to continually develop to (theoretically, at least) stay one step ahead of smaller competition.

Tier 2: Challengers and Designer Labels

Challengers are the firms positioned just behind the Market Leaders but which, because of sound strategic and infrastructural investments, are making significant strides towards the Market Leaders.

Designer Labels tend to display the same behaviours and the same levels of credibility as the Market Leaders, but only within the limited sectors or practice areas in which they have chosen to specialise.

Tier 3: Bulk Suppliers, Local Heroes, and Endowment Firms

Bulk Suppliers are the firms who can, to be blunt, 'pile it high and sell it cheap'. Their strategy is to do a higher volume of work at lower margins to satisfy the less sophisticated clients, specialism-wise, but those clients for whom the price point is the most important purchasing factor.

Local Heroes are the firms who display the same behaviours and inspire the same loyalty as the Market Leaders, but do so on a regional or even single-city basis.

> Endowment Firms live on their history to sustain their position and profitability, and tend to be heavily reliant on 'doing what we've always done' to sustain their established clients' loyalty.
>
> **Tier 4: Utility Players and Agglomerations**
> Utility Players tend to be medium-sized firms operating on a local level who offer a broad client base a broad range of services. While, from a marketing perspective, the Utility Players tend to look fairly similar to each other – particularly to lay clients – other than having strong individual client relationships and a convenient location.
>
> Agglomerations tend to come into being following the consolidation of a number of local firms who have decided to bulk up through merger or acquisition in order to make a bigger splash in their local market.
>
> **Tier 5 – Minor League**
> These are the small and medium-sized firms that populate the various local markets that make up the national legal industry. Again, there's little to differentiate these firms and their proposition tends to hinge on their location/convenience, local knowledge, and local connections, as well as the price point they're able to offer.

While I do see merit in this model (hence its inclusion) and do introduce it to clients from time to time because I think it provides a very straightforward illustration of the legal market because of the very self-explanatory pen pictures it gives the different types of firms it covers, there are reasons I would never use it without admitting a note of caution.

The main reason for injecting that note of caution is the instant denigration using five tiers can cause. Immediately, people ascribe less value to tiers three, four, and five, whereas in reality there is very much a place for all of the types of firm the model covers. Personally, I also find that this obvious streaming is reinforced by the names used, which to me could be construed as a bit disrespectful (Bulk Suppliers, Endowment Firms, Utility Players) and one (Minor League) that is downright disparaging.

The truth of the matter is there is a market position for every type of firm, and there are potential clients for all of them. By defining which position you currently occupy, and which position you want to enjoy in the future, you can make sure your firm is positioned correctly and is offering – in the words of Mr Ogilvy – what your product is and who it is for.

Once you make that connection – and, of course, publicise it effectively – it will make it easier for you to achieve and maintain the position you want and, by extension, generate the types of clients and levels of fees you want for your firm.

What is a brand and, in real terms, what does 'brand' mean for a law firm?

In the legal market there is (and I am of course speaking very generally) a misconception that 'brand' is something to do with your logo, your strapline, or your corporate colours. Although you could very well employ any or all of these things to bring your brand to life, these things don't represent the substance behind your brand.

A brand is, basically:

- The way your market understands and thinks about your firm when your name comes up in conversation or enters their eye-line; and
- The personality they believe your firm has, and the image you portray in terms of quality, credibility, delivery, and (ultimately) satisfaction and success.

Also, given your brand is built around what you would like the public perception of your firm to be, it has to be inextricably linked to your client value proposition. You have already worked out exactly what you want to convey in terms of the advice and services you want to deliver, and how your advice and support will benefit your chosen markets and client groups. If you pursue the creation of a brand, that brand has to follow in step because the core elements of your client value proposition are the very things you want your clients, contacts, and prospects to feel every time they come across you.

Theoretically, what part does branding play in the positioning process?

There is no doubt that positioning and branding are interlinked, but they are different.

If we go back to David Ogilvy's definition of position, once you get 'what your product does' in front of 'who it is for', your brand is how you are perceived by that audience.

When it comes to creating a successful brand there are almost as many schools of thought as there are schools, so let me distil the most notable characteristics down for you (see Figure 1 for a summary):

1. Recognition

Your name has to be known in your chosen markets. You need your name and your reputation to immediately resonate every time someone comes across you – in conversation, in print, or online.

Some of this will be tactical (are you advertising the right message in the right places, which relies on your deciding on the right client value proposition and the right market position). But some of it will rely on the 'word of mouth', having sympathetic and enthusiastic advocates willing to promote and reinforce your brand on your behalf.

2. Uniqueness

Yet again, I will nail my colours to the mast and say there is no point looking for your unique point of differentiation. However, there are other ways to articulate your uniqueness.

Say what your markets want to hear in the language they understand and using the reference points, trends, and angles that will reinforce your credibility. In many cases, taking this type of practical, relevant approach will be unique enough, particularly in seams where your competitors still insist on leading their marketing communications with legalisms and partner CVs in an attempt to engage their audience.

3. Passion

If your brand is going to spark a passionate reaction, you have to convey your brand with passion. You need to speak in bold superlatives and be prepared to stand by those superlatives. You also need to be able to convey those messages passionately in person, in writing, and online.

Figure 1: The seven elements of a successful brand

4. Consistency

A brand will never take root unless it is promoted consistently, and adopted consistently across every practice area and every marketing channel. You cannot afford to send out mixed messages or have one team adhering to their own idea of what the brand should be. Likewise, the decisions you take regarding promotional vehicles need to be consistent; for example, if your brand is based on cutting-edge modernity, you can't then communicate that message through billboard advertising and hard-copy newsletters.

Similarly, your clients want a consistency of service. If they get great service from your property and commercial departments but have a totally different experience when dealing with your employment team, the consistency of your brand will be called into question – and it is when questions arise that the client may consider seeking an alternative provider.

5. Competitiveness

Gaining a foothold in today's increasingly competitive legal market is no easy task. This is why you need to use your competition as a motivator rather than seeing it as a threat. Competition should drive your brand, your proposition, and your service offering, and it should enable you to be the very best firm you can be.

Similarly, don't close your eyes to what your competition is doing. Maintain a watching brief on new ideas, new services, and new delivery mechanisms, and be prepared to appropriate the best bits into your own delivery to ensure your firm remains a leader rather than a follower – or, worse still, an 'also ran'.

6. Exposure

If your brand is going to take hold the way you want it to, your exposure needs to be continual and as penetrating within your chosen market position as it possibly can be. You can't rely on sporadic e-bulletins or dipping in and out of local organisations or events; you need to be ready to embrace the 'little and often' ethos across your entire fee-earning community so that you are continually visible to your clients, contacts, and targets.

If you are serious about building a robust market position, you can no longer rely on excuses like, 'well, we're busy at the moment so even if we won a new client we wouldn't be able to resource their work'.

A maxim I often refer to when talking about this part of the positioning process with clients comes from Henry Ford who said, 'When times are good you should advertise, when times are bad you *must* advertise'. In the case of the legal profession, this means maintaining a profile in person, in writing, and online at all times. And if you're in any doubt as to the veracity of the sentiment, Mr Ford's company has done OK over the years!

7. Leadership

Every good PLC has a strong CEO. Every good company has a strong manging director. Every good football team has a strong manager. Therefore every good law firm needs to have a strong partnership (or working group within the partnership) who are going to commit not only to taking the firm's brand forward, but also to cementing the values ascribed to the brand within every fibre of the firm, and who will ensure that the recognition, uniqueness, passion, consistency, competitiveness, and exposure are adhered to and maintained.

What part does brand *really* play within the positioning process?

This may come as something of a surprise, but I would be inclined to suggest you actually steer away from spending too much time deliberating over your brand. If you were selling consumables or FMCG-type products, brand is an essential part of your story. In the legal world it can lead to an unnecessary level of complexity and – especially when the final responsibility for unravelling that complexity lies largely in the hands of legal rather than marketing professionals – the desire to find the perfect answer usually delays the launch, maintenance, and promotion of the messages you need to get out in your chosen markets, in order to sell your services.

My advice would be to concentrate on building the strongest possible client value proposition as this is the fundamental element to establishing a product, package, and position that will really help you kick on and profit from your efforts. In truth, using a strongly defined client value proposition to permeate your chosen market position is enough to succeed in a professional services environment. As long as you are saying the right things to the right people, that audience will extrapolate the personality traits you wish to convey and grow to react to your name as you want them to.

However, if you are dead-set on creating a brand, then my advice would be to leave it right until the end of the packaging/positioning process and follow this very simple three-stage model. (Illustrated in Figure 2.)

1. Create your client value proposition

This is what we do; this is why we do it; and this is how what we do will massively help you and deliver returns far in excess of the costs involved.

2. Decide on your desired market position

This is the level of the market we want to operate in; this is the part of the market we can leverage to grow; this is the position

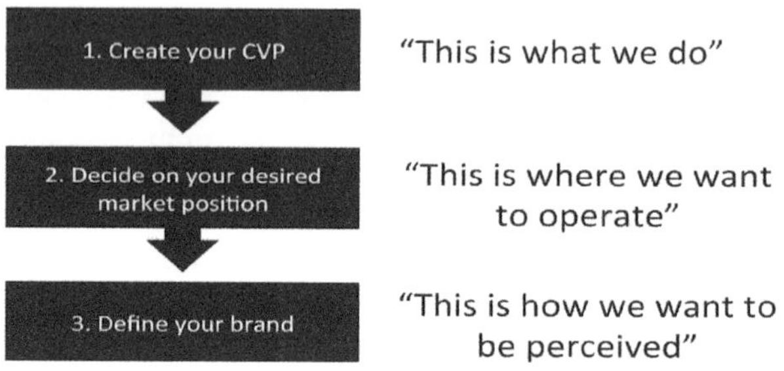

Figure 2: The packaging/positioning process

we can cement because of our location, specialisms, and price point.

3. Define your brand

This is how we want to be perceived; this is what we want people to think when they hear our name; this is why we are more credible, why we're a better choice, and why we will be a more successful partner for you than our competitors.

In the next chapter we will look at some specific examples of firms who have, in very different ways, attained the market position they wanted by choosing who they want to be and how they'd like to be perceived.

Chapter 6: Examples of packaging and positioning in today's legal market

We've worked through quite a bit of theory and looked at the practical steps you can take to package and position your firm so that it is more relevant and more attractive to your clients, contacts, and targets. At this point, I thought it might be useful to include some real-life examples so that you can see how other firms have approached the task of successfully developing the way they package and position themselves.

To do that, I spoke to a number of firms on both sides of the Atlantic; some I'd worked with, some I'd heard of, and some I found out about while I was researching this book. Rather than speaking to the managing partner and hearing the 'company line', I spoke to those closest to the projects they'd implemented so that I got a full, frank, and honest appraisal of what they did and what they have achieved.

For me, the results were fascinating. Not only was it good to see the innovative ways firms were refining their offerings, but also the similarities between the issues UK and US firms face – and the importance firms in both jurisdictions are placing on improving their offerings and their market position.

1. 'The sector specialist'

Interviewee: Ian H. Turvill, Chief Marketing Officer, Freeborn & Peters LLP

When it was originally suggested that I spoke to Ian during the writing of this book, I did (as you would expect) a little digging on his firm, Freeborn & Peters LLP.

During that initial due diligence, one of the things that immediately grabbed my attention was the firm's strapline, 'your future is our purpose'. I have already said that I don't place enormous stock in straplines; it is the core client value proposition from which the strapline comes that I feel is the fundamental part of any positioning exercise. That said, to me this strapline appeared completely consistent with the values and approach their website and marketing material promoted. More than that, it seemed to knit all of these things together neatly.

This is a slightly long-winded way of saying that, when I began speaking to Ian, I thought that the interview was going to major on where that line came from, how the firm embodied this message, and what the firm had done to make sure it delivered against this promise. We did touch on it, but organically our conversation took a slightly different and rather unexpected turn.

I have made no secret of my admiration for sector marketing and, more specifically, for those firms that get sector marketing right. It soon became apparent that Freeborn were almost certainly one of those firms:

> *'We wanted to be notably different in respect to the way we positioned ourselves. We had gone through the name change [placing emphasis on the first part of the firm name, Freeborn] and the rebranding. We wanted to look like we were expanding and dynamic and that, we hope, is embodied in the chevrons and sophisticated colour scheme from the rebranding process. We made sure all of those things were there in our offices in their full glory! It was a visual ID and focus that our clients immediately got and told us they appreciated. But we wanted more substance. Many of our partners have prior industry experience and we wanted to apply that experience to the way we looked after different clients, and use all of that to be much more than just corporate attorneys.'*

The firm's various sector foci were very clearly laid out on the website so I asked how they had come to the decision as to which they wanted to pursue:

'All of our work with sectors has been deliberate. Some came about because we had the credentials, the history, or some of the partners had the right CVs. Others were more serendipitous; some came to us and allowed us to add a bit of focus. For example, Food and Drink is historical; we've always done it. Healthcare just came to us when the ex-GC of HCSC Insurance joined us. Added to that, we now have very strong offerings when it comes to Private Equity/VCs and Transport which came about in their own ways. When it came to initiating our sectors, it took six or seven years of very formal effort but it has become pretty natural; it really is now a core part of our positioning.

'The primary reason we took the decision to use sectors rather than traditional practice areas was that we wanted to meet the needs of particular customers. We wanted to use our industry experience to differentiate us from our competitors. We wanted to build valuable intellectual capital – tell clients what's coming to bear and how best to deal with that. We wanted to tell them "we understand, let's build on that".'

The sector route having been chosen, the different specialisms needed to be promoted to the relevant client and target groups if it was to generate a financial return. I asked Ian how they achieved that traction:

'This was always going to be an important way of differentiating our offer, of differentiating us. But if we were going to show that we were offering totally relevant solutions to the sectors we'd chosen, it was evident there couldn't be one answer; every group was different. When it comes to Insurance, that isn't about broadcasting. It's about continuing to invest in direct relationships. Food and Drink is about intellectual capital, PR, points of view. It's about producing food safety news, local events – we are now synonymous with the

annual "Beer under Glass" event held at Chicago's Garfield Park Conservatory – and partnering with other professionals that specialise in the Food and Drink industries.'

Having discussed the positioning and packaging aspects, I turned to the most important question – has the focused, sector-led approach and investment in achieving specialist status in each area paid off?

'The client reaction has been very favourable. They know we genuinely understand their business. We know what's happening in that business and in that industry, and our clients know our appreciation of the circumstances and the issues means they are getting a better service and more proactive service. I am told repeatedly this is what is setting us apart – and ahead – of our competitors! Better still, it's led to referrals. Our clients are telling people about us, which of course makes our marketing more efficient and more effective.'

I ended by asking Ian what he thought would come next for his sector teams:

'In five years we'll review the list. That's the date on which we've agreed to make decisions on what works and what doesn't. Do we have the relevant expertise and interest? Do we have the right leadership? Do the teams look right? We know that if we can focus on the areas we know best, they will grow, but if we don't have that focus – or feel we have other areas we should be concentrating on – then we can't just let it play out as it is.'

2. 'The new market entrant'

Interviewee: Karl Chapman, Chief Executive Officer, Riverview Law

In seeking to illustrate the points this book makes about how to package and position a law firm, I knew that I had to talk to one of the UK's leading new market entrants. When I was offered an opportunity to talk to Karl Chapman, CEO of Riverview Law, I jumped at the chance.

These new businesses are going to be absolutely central to the way the UK (and, potentially, the global) legal market develops over the next few years. With this in mind, being able to gain an insight into how a company without a traditional law firm history has established a highly credible legal services brand was always going to be a hugely valuable addition to this section of the book.

The first thing Karl was at pains to tell me was:

> *'Riverview Law is not a law firm. It is a business, not a partnership. In my opinion, partnerships and law firms shouldn't exist in their traditional form, but they do. Our strapline is "Legal input, business output", and that's what we are here to do – to provide legal input that will deliver real value into our customers' businesses.'*

Karl then went on to tell me a little about Riverview Law's history:

> *'We are a technology-led business with deep legal domain experience. Riverview Law only exists because customers of one of our other businesses asked us to do their employment law work. We thought about it and realised that we could. However, we wanted to do it slightly differently; we wanted to provide a fixed-price model to give our clients total budget certainty. And, alongside the fixed fees, we wanted to provide all of the things you should get from a partner/supplier: comprehensive management information and reporting, monthly review and planning meetings, continuous improvement, proper project management.*

> *'We also wanted to use our technology and management information background to license that technology to*

customers to make their lives easier; to make everything more efficient for both parties. To me, this is one of the big trends: using data and technology to make the supply chain as effective and efficient as possible. However, we also realised that unless you *produce it, someone else will, so although we didn't anticipate doing so at the outset we now license our technology to customers and competitors through our technology subsidiary, Kim.'*

Notwithstanding the structure, approach, and technology underpinning the business, it was immediately apparent that Karl placed an even higher value on the people driving those elements:

'Our values are that we are always individual, enthusiastic, inquisitive, professional, positive, and act as one team. This is our DNA, in our personality, and they're all things we look for right from the recruitment process. And our client teams aren't just solicitors but also customer managers, project managers, data managers. One team with the ability to deliver everything the client needs to have so that they get that business output.'

As all of this was something of a new approach in the legal world (though, ironically, it is the approach that those amongst the corporate world who are reliant on direct client relationships adopted and implemented some time ago), I asked how it was received:

'The market wasn't nervous, they just didn't understand it so we had to explain how we can help, how it all fits together. We answered the question "so, what does it mean for me?" Our early adopters took a calculated risk and as that list of early adopters included names like Vodafone, Unilever, and HSBC, it became easier to persuade others

to follow. We also maintained real focus as we evolved our services and solutions to customers.'

'For example, we have regular (typically monthly) review meetings with customers, all based on a structured agenda, to discuss workflow and processes and again all of those meetings involve the whole team – the solicitors, the customer managers, the project managers, and the data managers – so that the client gets the highest possible value from each of those meetings.'

I finished the interview by asking Karl what he felt the future held for the legal market:

'Law has not been subjected to the competitive and costs pressures that most other functions and professional services have experienced over the last 25 years. It is about to become a very competitive industry. For me the biggest threat to law firms is the rise of in-house teams and their increasing ability to use technology to do many of the things that have traditionally been delivered by the supply chain. The accountants – especially the Big 4 – are another massive threat. They understand scale and they understand products. Admittedly, some law firms are doing things for their existing customers, for example Allen & Overy, Eversheds, DWF, and Pinsents. They are rightly challenging their existing delivery mechanism and their existing scales and they are making much more astute use of technology, but this needs to become the norm, not remain the exception. It is a great time to be in the legal business.'

3. Achieving growth through personal development

Interviewee: Jill Weber, Chief Marketing and Business Development Officer, Stinson Leonard Street

Jill Weber is the Chief Marketing and Business Development Officer at Stinson Leonard Street (a US firm that, following a

2014 merger, now has 450 attorneys across 13 offices). In 2004, Jill introduced an innovative programme designed to help an initial group of 20 attorneys grow their practices by $0.5 million each ($10 million in aggregate) in strict revenue terms within two years.

While the programme was ostensibly about accelerated revenue growth, it was also created to strengthen the individual attorneys' business development capabilities, as Jill explained when we spoke:

'The Fast Forward programme was designed to be an integrated BD programme to grow revenue in the near-term for partners with less than 10 years' experience. It was also meant to help build fundamental business development skills that would benefit the partners and the firm for years to come.

'Originally, the programme was made up of 20 partners, all of whom we recognised had high potential but who didn't at that point have significant books of business. We set specific revenue goals. Initially, everyone had the same target – $0.5 million in two years – but we've now recognised one size doesn't fit all so there are different targets for different people. The setting of such specific financial goals was interesting in itself. Most law firms don't set specific revenue goals at the individual attorney level; instead, they focus on individual billable hour goals. To us, revenue had to be an essential part of the programme's target setting.'

So, once the group had been decided and the targets given out, what was the next move?

'We asked all of the partners what type of relationship they wanted to have with their clients. The key was to get them thinking far beyond the transactional and adopting much more of a client service focus to help them identify

opportunities. We then gave them all of the support they needed – we provided them with one-on-one coaching, group training sessions, and even sales incentives. For example, we offered an awards trip that included three nights/four days for the partner and his/her spouse to any Ritz Carlton in the US, with airfares and childcare all included – a few of them were heavily motivated by that one!'

Given that a huge part of my day job is training and coaching partners and associates in law firms, I was interested to find out more about the selection criteria Jill employed for the coaches:

'We wanted specific legal experience, a long history of working with law firms and – wherever possible – a long history of working with our firm as that would give them a sound working knowledge of our culture. When we spoke to the coaches' references, we asked those references to describe the specific impact the coach had on revenue, not just how they changed business development behaviour.'

While the coaches did naturally play a pivotal part in the personal development of the partners involved, there was also an internal learning mechanism that was equally important to the success of the programme, as Jill went on to explain:

'Once we chose a coach, we would assign quantifiable revenue goals, by year, to each partner, and then asked them to focus on specific clients. The coach would guide them through that process, helping them approach it from the client's perspective and what the client most needed to achieve their business goals. At the same time, we offered monthly educational sessions to allow the partners to swap stories and experiences so they built not only their own confidence but also built trusted relationships with their colleagues. It gave them the confidence to cross-sell services because they knew the people from the other

practices personally through these lunches and other group activities. Building relationships across multiple offices and disciplines was absolutely essential. We found they really did learn from each other.'

The proof, as they say, is in the pudding, so how did the first two-year programme end?

'At the end of the first programme, the participants grew their practices by $7.5 million; we invested $150,000 in programme costs. I'd call that a success! Our programme components were guided by statistics from a BYU [Brigham Young University] study on how to maximize the retention of knowledge from training, i.e. it goes up to around 90 per cent when the learning is written down and you create personal accountability through follow-up by another person (i.e. the coaches).'

At this point, I can almost hear some readers saying that all of this is a great idea but surely it is more about traditional BD and personal development than it is about positioning. I disagree. I left our conversation thinking that all of the tweaks being made to the way various partners package and present themselves and the drive towards a more fluid, more closely interlinked offering across the firm that would support greater volumes of cross-selling are central to the way the firm wanted to position itself.

As Jill continued, it was soon apparent that all of the work she'd done had brought her team closer to their respective markets and that is a strategic shift that had to directly influence their clients' view of them as a firm, and as more than 'just lawyers':

'We started providing [the participants] with daily news feeds from which they could identify opportunities to reach out to their clients. We made sure they got closer to their

clients' businesses and visited clients in person – and they always came back with work! For example, we won a new client because one of the Fast Forward participants saw a news article that a GC he knew had moved. He got in touch and offered to go and see him in his new post but he also brought along colleagues who were recognised experts in his new industry. Of course, the client wanted to learn what they had to share and we wanted to provide those resources!'

More importantly, it appears the clients recognise all of the efforts the firm is making on their behalf, and client feedback from in-person and electronic surveys the firm conducts verify this conclusion.

'Clients tell us our attorneys understand their industry, that we've assembled just the right team for them, that we spend time with the client, that the attorney invests the time to visit "off the clock" and is ready to quarterback for them. We have instilled the need to know your clients' business and a good example of that is the employment lawyer who offered a packaged affirmative action plan audit designed to address feedback received from clients.'

For me, Jill's closing anecdote distilled not only everything her firm has tried to achieve via Fast Forward, but also just how successful those efforts have been:

'One client said he knew he could conduct an RFP and might find a different lawyer at a different price, but that would be a massive risk because Lawyer X (our guy) knows their business, knows the people, and knows how to communicate with those people involved – and all of that is worth far more than any discount.'

Quod erat demonstrandum, as legions of Romans and generations of amateur mathematicians may well have said....

4. Creating a truly exceptional client experience

Interviewee: Angela Hickey, Executive Director, Levenfeld Pearlstein, LLC

At the end of Chapter 3, we touched on the CVP Angela Hickey has created for Levenfeld Pearlstein and the fact that CVP is inextricably linked to their website's declaration that 'doing good legal work isn't what we aspire to – it's where we begin'. My conversation with Angela picked up where this declaration left off.[1]

Right from the start, Angela told me that in the highly competitive Chicago market the firm needed to say something different – and to actually *be* different – if it was to position itself as different to the other firms out there. The crux of that message had to be based on understanding (of their clients, of their needs, of the various local markets their clients operated in), and on the strength and closeness of their relationships.

From that conclusion grew 'The LP Way', a five-step programme designed to deliver the firm's competitive strategy: an exceptional experience for clients. By way of background, it is probably worth listing out those five steps before we get into the meat of my interview with Angela:

1. Attract and retain talent;
2. Lead by example;
3. Cultivate effective groups;
4. Align systems; and
5. Ask for feedback.

Goal: Unparalleled client experience

Once those steps had been explained, I began by asking what were the first steps the firm took to implement their idea:

> *'The most difficult step was creating effective practice groups. As a firm we're really lucky because we have a high*

level of engagement from our leaders who demonstrate total commitment to achieving client experience excellence, so we had the framework we required to put The LP Way in place. At other firms there's always the challenge of attorney attrition and then little progress is made. Because of our partners' longevity, this was built to last from the start.'

And from the start it quickly became apparent that the partnership was keen to implement The LP Way for very strong commercial reasons:

'All of our partners understood that just saying "we are quality lawyers" won't distinguish us. The "must have" for clients is the exceptional experience, so instead of concentrating on the legal side we decided rather to concentrate on the CX [client experience] and to deliver the best CX we could build. We knew if we could get it right we would create super fans and super fans would create referrals and referrals would create revenue growth.'

Angela was experienced enough to know that to find this level of client experience, she would have to seek advice from outside the legal profession:

'Most best practices for strategy execution are outside of the legal industry and if this was going to work it was necessary to build structure for a client experience. Many firms say they deliver great client service but without structure, it is impossible to consistently deliver. We wanted to offer "big firm" legal expertise at a greater value by making the client experience our number one priority.

'I think it's fair to say that each client's expectations are a little different but every client wants excellent client service so we looked at the very best experiences from the corporate

world and studied why they were the best. What we learned is that there is an important distinction between client service and client experience; the former is transactional and the latter is rooted in meaningful relationships. We then took the best bits we could find from the corporate world – from organizations like Disney and Ritz Carlton – and built a comprehensive structure. For example [US department store] Nordstrom actually openly gives customers the autonomy to make decisions as to how to improve their shopping experience and have generated ideas like if a customer returns an item they receive a $50 gift voucher for their trouble. Who isn't going to tell their friends about that? Suddenly, a potential negative, the return, is turned into a positive, the voucher! Transparency and decentralized decision making are key tenants of The LP Way.'

Identifying the strategic need for an exceptional client experience, deciding upon exactly how that exceptional client experience should look, and securing senior buy-in to support the implementation is no mean feat, but there was still the question of the actual implementation to manage. How did Angela achieve that?

'We began by establishing a common language that all employees of the firm could understand. Everyone in the firm understands the five steps of the LP Way. We then provided support tied to evaluation, compensation, and management. Once that was in place we moved internal language away from client service and fixed all of our focus on experience instead. Also, we introduced new metrics and stopped managing by traditional metrics such as the billable hour. We made sure people felt good about driving a good experience for their clients.'

All of this took considerable time and resources to implement, not to mention the seismic cultural shift required to make it work so my next question was the obvious one, 'Has it worked?'

'Well, our financial performance has enjoyed a strong upward trajectory where the industry reports flat growth. I cannot yet prove that is a direct result of The LP Way but there's a strong correlation. My next task is to prove that the positive performance trend is as a result of the LP Way. The one thing I can point to is the client feedback we have received. We are now hearing things like "I can't believe you're a law firm", "I could never leave you now", and "you're our strategic partner". If it's going to succeed, a law firm needs something more substantial than the fragility of relationships. We have to listen to clients and create the right tools for them, we need to improve our communications and the distribution of our services, and to do that we've created new tech-based extranet tools that are super bad ass!'

I ended by asking what will come next:

'Our job is not to just provide legal advice but to keep finding out exactly where our clients' frustrations are. We need to understand and help solve their business challenges; we need to provide a greater update frequency and make sure our clients don't have to keep chasing us down for things. All of that is made easier now that we've established the type of relationship only an exceptional client experience can deliver. I truly believe we have established a culture of transparency and sharing both internally and with our clients.'

Additionally, according to Angela, the benefit for the client is not limited to a better level of service and more open dialogue between attorneys and their clients:

'We are making many business introductions and connections for our clients simply by having a better understanding of who their targets are and then utilising the firm's entire network in an attempt to get our clients in front of those targets. It has been a knowledge management exercise that's taken us over a decade of work to establish but now we are in a position where we can find clients the right people to meet.'

5. Deep sector understanding and the capacity to deliver it the way clients demand

Interviewee: Roger Inman, Partner and Head of the Education Team, Stone King LLP

Stone King's fast-growing national practice in the UK is roughly broken down into four parts – education, charity, business, and private client – and is serviced from their offices in London, Bath, Cambridge, and Leeds.

Although it is ranked as a top-tier firm in the education and charity sectors, my understanding was that education was a relatively recent addition to Stone King's offering. Despite their late entry into this market, their leading position suggested they must have worked hard to package and position their offering, which is why I asked to speak to Roger Inman, head of their education team. I began the interview by asking the obvious question: how (and when) did Stone King get into the education sector?

'We go back a long way as a firm, to 1785, and during the first two centuries of that time we built up a solid practice in the South West as a quality provincial law firm and it was that reputation that persuaded some of the public schools in our local area to appoint us as their lawyers. But if we're talking about developing a real education practice, we didn't really do anything really substantial until after 2000. We recognised state schools were about to grow into a sizeable marketplace so we hired Richard Gold, a very well-known expert in voluntary aided schools. At that

point we probably had about 40–50 schools as clients and we were known as "good guys" but we didn't have any real focus. We could see there was potential in the education marketplace but we had no marketing plan, just a feeling there was an opportunity!'

I then asked Roger how the team went about turning that potential opportunity into the commercially successful team it is today:

'We developed a proposition. We knew we needed to develop a way of working with clients that suited those clients; that provided what they wanted in the way they wanted it. We developed a holistic approach based squarely on our sector knowledge. What we wanted to do was combine the lawyer with a head teacher to show them how to run a school more effectively, and to do that we distilled all of our sector knowledge and used that to generate credibility around us in the market.

'The first step was to create our new CVP (client value proposition) and that built up from our deep sector knowledge but we also knew we had to turn that knowledge around fast for our clients if they were to get the maximum benefit from it. This gave us our core proposition – knowledge, understanding, response, turnaround – a simple set of ideas which said what we had and how it would benefit school leaders.

'We then looked at the packaging: what was the best way to deliver our sector knowledge? From the start, we looked longer term. We wanted to glue clients in, get closer to them, so we developed our fixed-fee retainer options. There were no restrictions on the number of matters a client could ask about, and they knew how much they got free and exactly when the time-recording would start if things needed to be

progressed. It was a great way of making sure clients stayed in regular contact with us.'

This takes us up to the time the leadership of Stone King's education team passed from Richard Gold to Roger Inman:

'I was lucky when I took over the team in 2008. The building blocks were in place, our people were in a routine, they all had regular access to clients but unfortunately they still had the close focus of lawyers and largely speaking there was no overall strategy and no real interest in increasing the volume of clients beyond organic growth.

'Somewhat fortuitously, that was when academy conversion came in. We already had an established academy specialism working for some of the 300-odd sponsored academies setup before 2010. Then the Academies Act of 2010 allowed schools to convert to academy status and, better still, offered a financial incentive to do it. We knew this was a huge opportunity for us. They presented a brand new sector and a brand new marketplace for us. I don't know what the marketing equivalent would be because brand new markets don't come along very often. Maybe mobile phones? I can't think of another one.

'However, we knew we had to respond. So phase one – which was probably 2010–2013 – saw so much work coming in that we had to stop taking on new work for a period to avoid overtrading, which is a disaster for professional service firms. We knew that once things died down a bit and that first wave was over, we needed to build a machine. If we were going to compete and provide the best possible service for our clients, we needed to concentrate on increasing our capacity and building our expertise. So we developed our existing team to meet this opportunity. Most of our capacity growth took

place, however, because we were approached by several of our competitors who liked what we were doing and came to talk to us, which allowed us the double benefit of taking on both teams and market share from our competitors.'

'All of these bolt-ons stuck and became invaluable. In the first seven years they helped us reach critical mass and gave us the numbers, the capacity, we needed to attract the rest of the schools looking to convert to academy status and the volume of clients we wanted, and I'm very glad to say we were able to achieve that. And while there are still more academy clients coming in, I think it's fair to say the best clients – the client profile we really wanted – were in that first harvest. It is the entrepreneurs in education that are already in the academy space and see the value of working with specialist lawyers. We also have picked up academy clients from other non-specialist firms after academy conversion, when the client needs specialist education law advice to meet an operational need. That is where the knowledge and understanding kicks in – and of course the capacity to provide the response and turnaround the client has to have to operate.'

As it looks as through Stone King's proposition has been set and the team has brought in the capacity and specialist expertise required to deliver on the promises that make up the proposition, I was interested to find out what phase two might look like:

'The object is to convert our transaction-led growth through academy conversions into long-term clients. At present, we want 60 per cent of our regular work to come from our established clients to reduce our dependency on the set-ups and conversions. We want to integrate our clients into our full-service offering, which means we have to follow a three-step plan:

1. *Manage the conversion process;*
2. *Retain the client – and this is where the deep sector knowledge is vital, this is where other firms offering an academy service without having that knowledge and understanding simply can't survive;*
3. *Extend the relationship and keep adding value.'*

While that all sounded like complete common sense to me, how was the team planning on achieving those aims?

'By maintaining and growing our clients. Internally, this means a complete refocus on CRM (client relationship management), on KYC (know your clients), all the things that allow you to maximise your client relationships. Externally, it's about keeping developing that strong CVP and making sure the message is out there and understood by our market. At the end of our first phase of academy growth, we had no marketing collateral (no brochure, in fact) and no real BD structure and strategy in place. It was something we couldn't do when we were in the middle of the initial conversion maelstrom. Then we were too busy to do any real marketing, we just couldn't tie our people down. We have it all in place now and it's paying off.

'Since the 2015 [UK general] election, we have continued to invest internally in our relationship strategy and it's taking root. Externally, we are promoting our CVP heavily in our collateral, in our thinking because we get it into people during their inductions, in the way we approach events, even in the way we describe ourselves. And we are using structured client service review programmes to repeatedly check we are doing what we're supposed to be doing, and to find out more about what our clients consider to be real added value and how we can deliver that better.

'All of this has to come together because we are unashamedly going for the quality end of the market – we are pushing to achieve a good share of the people that are prepared to buy law because they understand the value of it. Yes, some of it has been down to luck rather than judgement, but quality people have come to us and the team now includes a quarter of all the lawyers with national individual rankings as education specialists in Chambers legal directory.'

As Roger was positive about the team's proposition and people, I then asked what he thought their market position currently is:

'If you look at the market in terms of everything from rocket scientists to full commoditisation, we're not rocket scientists but we are – I believe – in the next category along – and anyone who can occupy that particular space should grab it with both hands! That's where I think we are and I am confident we are in a position where we can be happy to exchange volume for quality and margin.'

I ended by asking Roger what were his plans for the future:

'No one knows the threat of AI and things like that, but you can't sit on your hands worrying about these things. Stay abreast of them yes, work out how best to use them, yes, but it can't be used as an excuse to prevent progress. Our plan is to keep quality as the keystone of all we do while completing our national footprint in England. We want to establish a full market footprint – not on a "stack 'em high" basis, but by filling the national space with a quality offering – and to have the right people coming through to ensure our succession keeps us at the forefront of the education sector long into the future.'

6. The right people, the right reputation, the right skills – promoted in the right way

Interviewee: John Seigal, Managing Partner, Clintons

Clintons are an internationally recognised leader in Media and Entertainment Law. Their long-established client base of instantly recognisable names from the entertainment world ensures they continue to not only maintain their market-leading position, but also continue to develop into new areas while sustaining an enviable level of profitability.

As part of the research for this book, I met with Clintons' Managing Partner, John Seigal, to find out how the firm has managed to hold its traditional position while at the same time broadening out its service offering and maintaining the level of profitability the partners demand.

I started with the obvious question: how do you maintain your position as an internationally recognised market leader? John's answer was simple:

> *'It's all down to the people. All of our people are trained by the best and that is a perpetual cycle. Over the years we've got a good feel for what makes a good lawyer and we do everything during our recruitment process to make sure we stick to that so that we only bring in lawyers we think will make the grade and stick with us for the duration. I am very proud of the fact we have never lost an equity partner to a competitor.'*

John couldn't be clearer about why it is so crucial to keep the people at the heart of the firm's proposition:

> *'We get the biggest deals going because of the brand. Because our people are at the very top of their game, our name is always being bandied around. We don't need to change that – just keep it going. Our proposition is simple: it's the people, the service, and the expertise.'*

When it comes to bringing in the right people, John explained it's as much about attitude, passion, and a genuine love for the industry as it is about academic results:

'Yes, if someone comes in we can train them, but it's a slow process and there are no short circuits. We need to know these people are going to be out there, that they're going to keep their ear to the ground and know what's going on. Straight from being a trainee, people have to know what's expected of them. For example, at the moment we have one [a trainee] who listens to 100-plus new bands a month and makes playlists of who we should be aware of – that is demonstrating the right attitude and the fact they know where to look for new opportunities. They have passion and a love for their industry; you can't train that.

'But this isn't just relevant to new recruits or junior lawyers looking to make their mark. All of these traits need to be demonstrated by the more senior fee earners in the firm – those who are recruiting and training the new blood. Again, whether you call it your proposition, your personality, your offering, or your brand, consistency is absolutely key to your success.'

And when it comes to the most effective way for a market-leading firm to promote their proposition, John was equally straightforward:

'Don't shout it from the rooftops! We don't use PR, we have a low-key website, we don't use direct mail, and £20,000-tables at industry events are a waste of time. The best vehicle is just having lunch or a drink with the people we need to see. We also maintain a profile at the major industry events at home and overseas so we see who we need to see and get seen by those who need to see us.'

And when it comes to the objectives for this type of business development activity?

> *'For people [potential clients] confidence comes from results; that's what makes people make decisions. That confidence will only ever come from a continual flow of top-notch people with the right expertise who promote that expertise in the right way.'*

With regards to broadening out the firm's traditional Media and Entertainment-centred offering, the most recent additions have centred on nothing more complicated than strategic organic growth, something John referred to as just 'finding the right people'. However, because of the firm's position they admittedly have the luxury of being able to afford to wait for the right person to come along.

The most recent additions to the firm's offering have been:

1. Film and TV

Given the firm's historic links to the worlds of media and entertainment, the partners had long considered the addition of a film and TV practice to be a logical and natural adjunct. However, they were not prepared to take just anyone; they had to find exactly the right person so the balance of the partnership wasn't affected in any way.

Without putting any real feelers out into the market, Clintons were approached by a very well-known figure within the world of film. He had already built a great reputation and was extremely highly regarded. More importantly, he had also done his homework and realised Clintons was the right firm for him to continue to grow his practice. John explained:

> *'He was ready to get stuck in from the off. He brought experience and contacts and used them to create a template for himself. Because of the way he wanted to work, the*

environment was conducive [to success]. Clintons is a known brand and he just positioned himself within that brand by being completely entrepreneurial – something he knew because he'd done his homework and due diligence – which allowed him to build his department from scratch exactly the way he wanted it to be.'

The firm's film and TV practice continues to grow apace and over the last two years it has grown from just that one partner to a team of three, including a senior assistant and a solicitor who recently qualified via the Clintons training programme.

2. Employment

Employment work used to be something the firm's lawyers did piecemeal across the board, but the partners recognised their approach was a little disparate and, given the importance of the work they were doing for their existing clients (a lot of which was 'for senior music execs who were on big numbers and big contracts'), they knew there was a need to strengthen their offering, and that would require the lateral hiring of a high-standing employment specialist.

Because they placed such an enormous importance on finding exactly the right people to join their team, Clintons had a retained agent who had established their credibility by bringing in a number of very high calibre candidates. They had taken time to get to know the firm and recognised this was way beyond a standard recruitment sales job to fill seats. They knew they had to be prepared to spend as much time as necessary to find exactly the right fit and that if that fit wasn't there, the firm wouldn't entertain a first meeting.

Having spent literally years trying to find the right person to head Clintons' new employment practice, the right candidate finally came along. The agent found a name that was recognised by peers in employment circles, but also someone who understood and fitted the firm's culture and had obvious potential despite having hit a glass ceiling in their current role. Again, their practice continues to go from strength to strength and further growth is scheduled for this year and beyond.

Having looked at how the firm continues to work hard to retain its position at the very forefront of media and entertainment law, and how they have enhanced their offering by diversifying in a logical and linear way, my conversation with John turned to the future. How did Clintons plan to continue to package and promote themselves in a way that would allow them to continue to profit from their market position?

> *'The future? Who knows! But one thing's for sure, our future success will be based on the personal not the structural. We won't overstretch, we don't want to conquer the world. We know what we're good at and we know how to deliver it. That will be at the heart of our future development.'*

One area – though geographical rather than industry- or sector-led – John has identified for growth is the United States and, in particular, Los Angeles:

> *'One thing we will do in 2017 is open in America. This is based purely on "invited exposure"; we have American clients and they're doing American deals so we'll go in under the radar to do their work and give them the level of service they need without attracting too much attention.'*

While it was refreshing to have such a positive conversation with a managing partner given the unrest and uncertainty that currently surrounds the UK legal market, I ended by asking John, given the percentage of the firm's income that is derived from the music business, did he think the wholesale changes continually reshaping the way that industry delivers its product to consumers could pose a threat to future fees?

'Listen, we saw LPs go to CDs, then there was a brief interruption from minidisk and then a move to downloads, the internet, and streaming. We stayed close to our clients, to our business, and made damn sure we understood exactly how to deliver for our clients whatever was going on. We just stayed out there and got our heads round it. It's their industry and it's always going to be reinventing itself, but however music is delivered, it's really just another income stream. We serve that industry so we need to adapt to it. In the future, we may look more closely at other genres: jazz, dance, classical. Did you know country and western has been the biggest genre by sales in the USA? Maybe that's something we should consider?'

John ended our conversation with a nugget of wisdom that I agreed with so vehemently, something that sums up what every law firm needs to strive to do irrespective of their size, specialism, or location so perfectly that I'm going to end this chapter with it:

'The legal business isn't complicated. You get the work because you're out there and you have a reputation for having the right expertise. You do the work, you bill for the work, then you make sure your bills are paid promptly. Too many firms make it all far more complicated than it needs to be!'

Reference

1. A more comprehensive case study entitled 'The LP Way – A revenue growth strategy' can be found in Growth Strategies for the Modern Law Firm published by the ARK Group in 2016; for further details you can also visit the LP website at www.lplegal.com.

Chapter 7:
How to price your services

There are many pricing specialists helping the legal market. I am not one of them. I do, however, believe that pricing is a central element of the marketing mix. After all, if you've gone through the process of refining your client value proposition and packaging your firm in the way that best fits the market position you want, all of that work will be wasted if you come up with a pricing structure that contradicts your message.

From a marketing perspective you have to ensure your pricing (in terms of the levels and the mechanisms) is congruent with your offering and the level of the legal market in which you operate.

How do you come up with your pricing model?

The first question to ask yourself is what is the best way to determine your pricing? If we look at this in the most straightforward terms, there are arguably only four ways to come up with a pricing model:

1. Cost-plus pricing

In many ways this is the easiest (and most traditional) way to price legal services. You know roughly how much it costs to do a piece of work (the level of fee earner required to do the work, the amount of more senior supervision that may be required, and the hourly rate you want to recover on each of those interventions). You then balance that out as an average hourly rate and add a margin to that rate so it generates a level of profit for the firm.

2. Competition-based pricing

If you are close to your market (whether that market is an industry sector or your region), you will have a good idea of roughly what the other firms marketing to your audience are charging. This insight will allow you to benchmark against (and perhaps even undercut) your competitors so that you remain a highly competitive option for your clients and targets.

Many firms are trying to come up with different ways of gleaning this insight. I have seen mystery shopping exercises and even partners masquerading as prospects in order to get a quotation for a specific piece of work. Neither of these exercises sits comfortably with me. I think that talking to your market and your clients should give you a good idea of what's going on and how your competitors are pricing themselves without having to resort to these types of campaigns.

3. Value-based pricing

Instead of looking at the time and resource required to deliver a piece of work, value-based pricing looks at how valuable the client perceives the work to be, i.e. the more valuable it is to them, the higher the price for it can be.

Although it can be applied to any practice area, it is probably most appropriate for firms and lawyers who have a recognised position as a leading luminary in a particular niche or where a lawyer has a very particular set of specialist skills that few others can offer.

4. Market-based pricing

Many firms now use their clients' – i.e. the market's – acceptance of an hourly rate as the benchmark of an acceptable pricing model. If firms use this model, they have to be very careful as they strike a balance between raising their fees as high as possible without raising them to a level that will make their clients move their work to a competitor.

My view is this is the least effective pricing methodology because it forces firms to overcharge in a weak market and undercharge in a strong market, which means there is no real consistency for a client and no opportunity to underline the value of the advice you are providing because it is charged at continually varying rates.

The other risk to maintaining a market-based pricing model is that most firms still operate within a discount culture. Fee earners are quick to discount their rates rather than support them, which means clients know they can take full advantage and push for those discounts. Not only will this have an effect on your revenues, it is actually more damaging as the additional time required to 'play the game' will have a cumulative impact on chargeable time.

Although there are only four accepted models upon which to base your fee levels, you can of course combine several if you think that would make your pricing more attractive to your target market(s) and more profitable for your firm.

Now take five...

Irrespective of whether you feel you follow a cost-plus, competitive, value-based, or market-based approach to pricing, choose one piece of work you recently completed and billed for and water-test the fee you charged by asking yourself:

- How much time and effort was actually required to complete the matter?
- Did you have all of the skills needed to complete the matter or did you have to bring in colleagues to help?
- How valuable was your work to the client (personally, strategically, or financially)?

- Was your original quote met positively or negatively?
- To the best of your knowledge, how did your proposed fee compare to the current market rate?

How will your clients react to your pricing?

As I've said repeatedly throughout this book, this is the most competitive legal market any of us has ever seen – and, as Karl Chapman noted in the previous chapter, it is about to become a *very* competitive industry. That means that although the pricing models we looked at in the previous section are OK in principle, can they really be considered relevant today?

When you are creating your value proposition, your messaging, your service offering, and the best way to promote and position your firm, you have to be looking directly at the client. You need to make sure:

- Your proposition is relevant to the clients you want;
- Your skills and expertise are what your clients need to succeed;
- You are delivering your services in the way that suits your clients best; and
- You are providing all of the added-value extras to make you not just the best option for, but invaluable to, your clients.

Taking all of that into consideration, does that not mean you should start your pricing discussion by looking at your clients and trying to work out what type of pricing they would respond best to?

Typically clients fall into four categories:

1. **Price-based clients:** You know these people. Price is the first thing they ask about and it tends to sit at the centre of any conversation you have with them.

2. **Relationship-based clients:** These are the clients who value the relationship they have with you (and your firm) above all else; as long as you don't push prices unrealistically high you can charge the rates you need to. Moreover, if you are a recognised specialist you may be able to increase those prices slightly as clients will be willing to pay to instigate a working relationship with you.

3. **Convenience-based clients:** In some practice areas immediacy and speed of turnaround are paramount so you are able to charge a premium rate to cover the provision of that speed of service; similarly, some clients may be willing to pay more for a 24-hour concierge style service or for home, international, or weekend visits at short notice during the busiest and most crucial times.

4. **Value-based clients:** Although this applies to all clients to some extent, these are the clients who will make a comparison to your competitors' fee levels, who may be shopping around a number of firms to find the best deal. However, on the flip-side, they are also the group who recognise and will respond to real added value, which means the inclusion of the right fringe benefits (training, response, accessibility, introductions, the provision of new opportunities) may sway their purchasing decision in your favour.

ACTION PLAN

Now take five...

- Work out which of these groups your clients fit into.
- Then think about which groups the clients you *want* fit into.
- Then discuss whether your current pricing levels match their profile or whether your prices are too high or, of course, too low.

- Again, this exercise will work as well for a department or a personal practice as it does for a firm.

How does your current pricing fit with the current state of your market?

Although clients are of course your main focus – and, therefore, your pricing model has to fit within their boundaries of acceptability – you also need to keep an eye on what's going on within your market.

What's going on in the market is a hugely valuable secondary yardstick against which to measure the fee levels you've decided upon. If you're massively out of kilter with the market at large, you may damage your credibility and unwittingly encourage your clients and targets to consider alternative options.

Traditionally, there are only three possible outcomes from your research:

1. You're priced about right

This, of course, is the outcome you're looking for!

2. You are overpriced for your market

The knee-jerk reaction to this outcome is all too often to panic and immediately reduce fees. That need not be the case. There is sometimes the potential to position yourself as the 'reassuringly expensive' option, but that strategy would have to be supported by particular and recognised specialisms or expertise, or by the fact you are the firm best equipped to support a new or high-growth industry within your market.

As a general rule of thumb, the clients who will accept an overpriced offering are either driven by relationship or convenience, and to maintain that perception you have to make sure your clients and targets know that you understand them implicitly. You need to make sure your marketing and messaging underlines your reputation as the 'go to' firm within your chosen markets so it is widely recognised that you can fulfil all of your clients' legal and service requirements.

3. You are underpriced for your market

In hugely competitive areas of the law (e.g. the 'high street' end of residential property, matrimonial, or personal injury) underpricing is an option. You need to compete with an increasing number of competitors vying for the same market – both in person and online – and the consumer for this type of product is undeniably positioned within the price-based group.

Moreover, you only need to meet minimum levels of expectation with regards to service, delivery, and turnaround and little value will be placed on the relative quality of your advice. It is more important that you do what you say you can do, at the best possible price (i.e. for less than the competition).

If you get your message and promotion right, this approach will definitely find a willing audience. Your only concerns should be that you can a) find a sufficient and consistent throughput of those types of clients and b) that you have the systems, controls, and processes in place to deliver the work in a way that generates sufficient and consistent profit.

4. You are 'competitively' priced

Alongside the three pricing strategies cited above, in a legal market that is increasingly basing itself on specialist foci rather than general practice, a fourth option growing in popularity is for firms to aim to be 'competitively' priced.

Competitive pricing plays directly to those firms or practices who boast very specific expertise for a particular niche. If you genuinely have that type of offering, you will neither want nor need to get into the pricing war. As with overpricing, your clients and targets will recognise that they will need to pay a premium for your specialist expertise but that premium is justified as the advice you provide will be more tailored, more focused, and more relevant. In turn, this should combine to provide greater effectiveness as well as greater time – and cost – efficiencies for your clients.

But you also need to factor in the greater awareness clients in a niche have around the price other potential suppliers are offering. Generally speaking the smaller the market, the more aware the market is of cost. You will need to stay aware of the pricing of your competitors because, while your specialisms will make you an attractive and credible option, you could lose out on opportunities if your pricing is above that of the handful of other firms who can offer the same specialist expertise and experience.

How do you charge for your services?

Traditionally (and by 'traditionally' I actually mean 'since about the 1960s') law firms have billed via the hourly rate. It is arguably a system that favours the law firm rather than the client, particularly as it is usually based upon 'blocks of time' of anything from 5–30 minutes, with anything delivered within a shorter timeframe rounded up under the 'or part of ...' caveat.

For years, the market accepted this means of billing even though clients were very quick to criticize when they received bills that showed something of an over-zealous approach to including every minute and more!

A combination of greater cost consciousness, resulting from the recent global recession, and more discerning and demanding clients aware of their ability to move work for better terms has seen a serious increase in the number of firms willing to discuss alternative fee arrangements (AFAs).

In the simplest terms, alternative or special fee arrangements are just the different ways a law firm and a client can come up with to find a mutually comfortable billing mechanism that isn't hourly based, and that both parties are happy with.

As far as clients are concerned, AFAs are not about charging more than they would expect to pay if they were working to an hourly rate. AFAs are about charging an appropriate fee for the work done against the value the client will derive from that work and/or offering greater budget certainty. It could well involve (or be based upon) the lawyer's hourly rate as a starting point, but it shouldn't be variable or inflated at any point if additional work is incurred during the progression of the matter at hand, unless periodic reviews and budget adjustments are a term of the original agreement.

Similarly, for the firm, AFAs aren't – as many firms fear – about charging less than they would be able to if they were 'on the clock'. It is about charging a mutually agreeable price for the work, irrespective of whether that work is completed in one, three, or five hours. If the client derives a certain level of value from the work, or if the work is business or time critical, that should be factored into the fee arrangement.

It is also important to note that retainer-style arrangements aren't AFAs. As retainers are usually based upon a monthly charge covering a certain amount of hours, this is really just an extension – though arguably more creative repackaging – of the good old hourly rate.

We looked briefly at some of the options you could consider if you are looking at introducing AFAs (or widening the range of AFAs you currently offer) earlier in the book, but it may be useful to recap those here, and also to provide a more comprehensive list of the options open to you:

1. A fixed or flat fee

This is the most basic alternative pricing mechanism. You work out a flat fee for a specific piece of work (or for the different components that you would expect to be involved) and offer that as a fixed rate.

This is particularly useful for the more everyday exercises you are involved in (drafting and reviewing) because you will have a pretty accurate idea as to how long these types of work typically take. Because of the human element, some will take longer than others but anecdotally I've been told that if you restrict these arrangements to the type of work you can predict fairly accurately, you will come out about even, if not a little ahead, by the end of the financial year.

The areas fixed fees are not particularly well suited to are the more contentious areas like civil or commercial litigation or family law where the amount of work can often be heavily influenced by the opposition's responses to your actions, responses that can be extremely hard to predict. However, some firms have introduced fixed fees on an 'up to a defined point' basis, at which point they switch to the hourly rate model.

2. A contingency (or success) fee

At the outset of a matter, the lawyer and client would agree a fee based upon clearly defined success criteria. Within the commercial world it may be exceeding a certain price level on the disposal of a business or the licence fee a client achieves when they licence a name, product, or process to a distributor.

In many cases this can be based on certain steps so that there is an added incentive for the lawyer to push the level of the deal as high as they can for their client. This can also be referred to as a risk/reward arrangement.

3. A percentage-based fee

This is pretty much the same as a contingent or success fee except the reward would be based upon a percentage of the amounts achieved for the client rather than on a definite flat or stepped fee.

4. Task-based billing

This type of arrangement allows firms to bill as the specific tasks involved in a matter are concluded, and the bills would only be sent out upon the completion of those tasks. This type of arrangement is particularly well suited to litigious actions where there are obvious cut-off points between the previous and next stages of a dispute. It affords clients a natural break in which to make the decision as to whether it is cost-effective and in their best interest to continue to progress the matter without incurring additional and unnecessary fees.

5. Retrospective 'value based' billing

This is a slightly tricky option to implement for some lawyers as the exact fee cannot be known until the work has been concluded. This is because the fee is based upon several pre-agreed factors (usually performance, outcome, and timeliness) and is usually tied to a rising scale depending on how well each of those factors has been met – and that discussion cannot, of course, happen until the matter has been concluded.

To add a little more complexity to the mix, you can also consider hybrid fee arrangements that borrow from a number of the ideas we've just looked at to form the billing model that best suits the client and their circumstances, for example:

6. Blended hourly rates

This is unashamedly based upon the traditional hourly rate system, but instead of listing out all of the hourly rates associated with each member or each level of lawyer within your team(s), you 'blend' this so you have an average rate you would charge across the board.

7. 'Fee collars'

These are also based on the hourly rate system but here the fees are bookended with maximum and minimum fees. In my personal experience, while this may look good on paper, it is the least popular with clients as they have no certainty as to where on the scale their fees will actually land.

8. Fixed fee + hourly rate

While it may be easy to offer a significant portion of the work required on a fixed fee, some of the work may be a little less certain, or even totally unforeseen. To combat that, the initial agreement may have to include some options that will need to be charged at an hourly rate.

One example of this model could be a divorce where the petitions and initial correspondence could be charged at a flat rate but where additional negotiation and even advocacy would have to be charged by the hour depending on the opposition's response. Similarly, in a commercial matter, contractual drafting and reviews could be charged at a flat fee but any contentious matters arising from the enforcement of those contracts may have to be billed on an hourly basis.

9. Fixed fee + success fee

This is a good model for situations where the lawyer(s) involved have a good level of understanding as to what the client needs, what they want to achieve, and the resources that were required to manage similar matters in the past.

Having that level of understanding will allow the transactional elements to be priced up accurately (which will make up the fixed fee part) and the likely risks associated with successfully concluding the transaction (which will inform the decision as to whether or not to offer the success-based part).

If this is the route you would like to propose then be very careful you have set out exactly what constitutes 'success', and exactly how and when the two elements will be billed.

10. Hourly rate + contingency

This is a good approach if you want to actively show your clients you are willing to share risk but, at the same time, as part of the fee will be based on a pre-agreed hourly rate, you will at least recoup part of your fee costs even if the worst happens and the contingency markers aren't hit. And if they are hit, you stand to make considerably more than you would by billing at a standard hourly rate.

Why should you consider implementing alternative fee arrangements?

As with many things in life, the thought of change can be more painful than the change itself. I think this is particularly true when it comes to law firms dropping the traditional hourly rate model and replacing 'what we've always done' with the AFAs clients are now expecting.

In a bid to alleviate some of the concerns around AFAs, I have set out the associated benefits below:

1. They increase profitability

Unfortunately, in many cases, the implementation of AFAs is a reactive move following a client request. That means that sometimes they aren't calculated as commercially as they should be. However, if you invest in the creation of AFAs that truly reflect the value of your services, cross-referenced with the time and resource required to deliver those services, AFAs will increase your profitability.

2. They increase client satisfaction

I know we've touched on the question of client satisfaction earlier in this book – several times in fact – but I can't underline heavily enough just how key happy clients are to a law firm's long-term success:

- Happy clients stay and if you keep your clients, real sustainable growth is easier to achieve;
- Happy clients are more amenable to cross-selling and up-selling approaches and if you can increase your clients' annual spend, real sustainable growth is easier to achieve; and
- Happy clients are more likely to refer you to their personal and professional networks and not only will these enquiries come with no cost of sale, they'll also be easier and quicker to convert as they've come off the back of a recommendation... making real sustainable growth easier to achieve.

The formula required to create the highest levels of client satisfaction is obviously a long and complex one. It involves getting every aspect of your technical and service delivery just right; however, it's worth persevering as AFAs will make an invaluable contribution by:

- Facilitating cost certainty – Clients value predictability in their legal costs as it allows them to budget more accurately; and
- Reducing the potential for misunderstandings – Disputes over legal fees and costs and the difficult conversations these misunderstandings can cause are still the number one reason clients decide to leave their current law firm and take their business to a competitor.

How do you decide which types of pricing suit you (and your clients) best?

Before you make any decisions on pricing and on how you bill, you need to do a full appraisal of what you need to do and why.

If you revisit your client value proposition and the work you have done on your positioning, you will have some insight into whether you should be following an overpricing, underpricing, or competitive pricing strategy.

If you have taken my suggestions regarding testing everything against your clients by implementing meaningful client review or client listening programmes, you will have a good idea how your clients view your current pricing and billing models (and maybe even an insight into your competitors' pricing and billing models if you've chosen clients who use a variety of law firms).

Client research will also give you a steer on what clients really consider to be added value and your willingness to adopt and promote those added-value items will help you support your fee levels when you're quoting or pitching for new work.

However, as price is usually the final piece in the somewhat complex jigsaw that is a client's decision-making process, you cannot afford to get it wrong. So, here are a few other things you may want to consider before you make your final decisions and, more crucially, make those decisions public:

1. Are you absolutely sure your pricing matches your clients' expectations?

Without sounding (too much) like a broken record, whether you are looking at product, promotion, package, or price, your clients views must come first. Get it right for your clients and the likelihood is all of the elements of your marketing and business development will be more likely to attract new clients and open up more cross- and up-selling opportunities within your current client base.

When it comes to pricing, ask yourself what your clients actually want from your services; generally speaking, this will be one or two things from the following list:

- A quick and/or easy resolution;
- A very specific outcome that will help them, their family, or their business;
- A positive impact on their finances or cash flow;
- Predictability for the future;
- Certainty for the future; or
- The setting of a precedent for the future.

While the importance of each will vary from client to client, there should be common themes and each element commands its own level of premium.

2. Do you have all of the information you need to ensure your pricing isn't just attractive externally but profitable internally?

Before you come up with a final pricing model, you need to be sure you know exactly:

- **Time**: How long does a specific piece/type of work tend to take?
- **Personnel**: Who is on the team? How big is the team? At what level is each member of the team?

- **Resource**: How much of the required time will fall to each member of the team?
- **Additional factors**: What else, other than time and people, will be required to complete the work?

3. Are you happy you are maximising every opportunity for internal leverage?

Aside from agreeing the overall fee, you also need to consider profitability. Profitability is easier to achieve if you can – wherever possible – push the work down to be done by either the lowest level capable of doing the work (so costs are as low as possible) or by the most experienced and capable person (so the speed of completion is as quick as possible).

Adopting this principle should, in theory at least, free up partner time for new business development activities which should win new opportunities that will in turn convert into new fees and increase profitability further.

4. Know the profitability pitfalls of offering even the smallest discount!

While a 1 per cent discount doesn't sound like much, many economists have irrevocably proved that even the smallest discount can have a greater impact on profit than you think.

If for simplicity's sake we say a lawyer completes a piece of work for £300, the general rule of thumb is that £100 goes towards their overhead, £100 goes towards their compensation, and £100 goes towards the firm's profit. Now if you discount that by 1 per cent the overhead and compensation requirement doesn't decrease, but the profit line takes an immediate 3 per cent hit.

If you get your pricing right and it is fully supported by your proposition, packaging, and market position, the level and frequency at which you need to discount (and that means using discounts solely to close, not to make yourself look like the 'good guy') will dramatically decrease.

What are the practical steps you need to take to put your new pricing model in place?

You could of course knee-jerk and bring in a specialist, but that could prove expensive and – in the case of a smaller or more focused/niche firm or for firms looking to tweak rather than to rip it up and start again – could conjure up images of nuts and sledgehammers.

Instead, try to follow this proven three-step plan:

1. Get blanket partner support

We all know nothing happens in a law firm without the full and unreserved support of the partnership so don't leave this to a conversation between your CFO/FD and the partner(s) or director/VP responsible for your marketing. Get full buy-in from partners by educating them as to why you need this new structure (and any new alterative fee arrangements you think would support your proposition) and how you arrived at the model you are introducing to them.

I've found from personal experience that showing how the new plans will positively impact on profitability (and therefore personal remuneration) never hurts!

2. Make sure all of your lawyers understand your pricing model (including any alternative fee arrangements)

Whatever pricing levels and models you come up with, your lawyers must understand them. Moreover, they also need to understand how you've come up with your pricing, why it needs to be adhered to, and the effects unnecessary discounts will have on your performance and profitability… and potentially their remuneration.

3. Make sure your systems meet all of your pricing requirements

It may sound simple to the point of obvious, but if you come up with the right pricing and a range of innovative fee arrangements but can't raise a bill accurately, easily, and in a timely fashion, it will affect the financial side of your practice.

Before you launch anything, make sure your systems and your processes can manage the administrative side. Then test your systems. Then test them again.

Added value and how to use it

Setting the headline cost aside, does your pricing really offer value? The only problem is, what does 'value' actually mean? I think it is fair to say it is a word that is used in a multitude of contexts in the legal profession and has a different meaning to pretty much everyone affected by or involved in each of those contexts internally or externally.

If your goal is to convince your clients, contacts, and targets that your firm offers a superior level of value to your competitors – and that should most definitely be one of your goals – you need to be absolutely sure of what 'value' is. The most accepted formula is:

Value = Benefits/Price

And in English? When clients are making their minds up as to the value of your offering, they are weighing up the benefits of your offer (for them) against the price you're proposing to charge. In their own way they'll compare your pricing to your competitors and then factor in their understanding of how you'll deliver your services and how your services will improve their lot.

If you are unable to articulate the additional value you offer (whether that's specialist expertise, innovative delivery mechanisms, or just the ability to deliver your services as quickly and easily as possible), you are forcing your audience to judge you on price alone and, unless your price is the lowest in your market, that could become a very difficult place to be.

Irrespective of which level of the market you want to occupy, my suggestion would be that it is always preferable to stay clear of the price-only end of the market. Instead, ensure you offer some recognisable form of added benefit to help clients recognise you offer them more than your competitors and that, by choosing your firm, they will obtain a higher level of value even though you may not necessarily be the cheapest option.

This is another pivotal factor when it comes to determining true added value. What you offer should not only allow you to raise your fee levels above the lowest point in the market, it should also allow you to justify the levels you propose.

However, as with most things in life, personal perspective tends to muddy the waters. For some, the highest level of value means cheap. To others it means valuable which, by extension, could very well mean expensive. In order to package and promote your added value in the way that supports your proposition you need to be careful you understand exactly how your clients and targets define value, then find the extras you would need to add over and above your legal advice in order to meet those expectations.

The whole concept of added value is a peculiar thing when it comes to marketing legal services. Far too many firms still consider 'added value' to be the continued provision of extras along the lines of 'what we've always done', whether that's running seminars, sending out an e-newsletter, or blogging about legal updates. However, true added value is about the 'value' part not the 'added' part.

As clients become more demanding in terms of what they expect from their different professional advisers, and more promiscuous in their purchasing behaviour (the nice way of saying more likely to move if their demands aren't met), if you genuinely want to inject value into your client relationships you need to find more ways than ever to boost the benefit your clients derive from working with you.

In turn, this means an irregular e-newsletter, the odd seminar, and an annual golf day no longer constitute added value. You need to be more creative, more practical, and more relevant in the design and execution of your added value extras.

The first step is to acknowledge one size definitely does not fit all in today's legal market. If you are going to build an added-value model that actually adds value, start by listing out what your clients (and remember, 'clients' includes contacts, referrers, and targets) actually consider to be valuable.

Some of this information can be gathered when your fee earners are out talking to your clients as part of their personal business development efforts. Some can be gathered via very short and simple client satisfaction questionnaires or via any of the online survey platforms now available. Some can be gathered as part of your annual independent client service review programme. And if you're thinking 'but we don't do an annual independent client service review programme', you need to think about starting one. How can you credibly market yourself as adding value if you're not asking clients what added value they want?

Your senior partners and marketing professionals can also help. Agree who are the top five clients in each practice area and task your senior partners or marketers with going to see them to ask what they want to see added on to your services. And if someone pulls a face at the potential investment required to deliver this, remind them the likelihood is that if it suits them, it will suit the majority of your clients, which means any insight you come back with will pay back in spades as it is rolled out to win new work from both current and new clients.

Once you have the results, the next step is easy. All you have to do is take a piece of paper and write down what your clients consider valuable down one side, and how you can deliver that information and/or those additional service levels down the other.

To help you get started, here is a list of some of the most successful initiatives I've been involved in:

1. Legal update seminars

Obviously, these are a mainstay of legal service provision, whether you are marketing commercial or private client services (or both). However, attendance at traditional seminars is dropping across the board so here are a few alternatives you could look at:

Electronic delivery

One of the reasons fewer people go to seminars is that they generally have less time. When that happens, it's the non-essential items that are first to go (with the irony being the updates you are providing are absolutely essential). If you film them – even using off-the-shelf 'slide and talk' options like GoToWebinar – you will build up a catalogue of shorts you can house in your media library or send out as mail pieces. Then people can watch them when it's convenient.

Smaller, more focused 'round tables'

Rather than running an old fashioned 'chalk and talk' style seminar, invite a smaller, handpicked audience and discuss the topics of the day. This allows you to be more relevant and gives people a more comfortable environment in which to ask about and debate what really affects them.

Evidence shows audiences draw much more value from this type of event as they're participating. It also gives them an opportunity to grow their network as there will be time to meet and get to know their peers, and even potential customers of their own, which is valuable in itself.

2. Repackage and revitalise your written content

Listicles

Just as your fee earners don't really have time to write 2,000-word dissertations any more, your clients don't have time to read them. While 'listicle' is without doubt an appalling word, the output is a very effective marketing tool.

By using a 'to the point bullet point' structure you can write and release '10 things you must remember when…' or '5 things you tend to forget when…' list-style articles quickly and easily. More importantly, as they're brief and to the point, people are more likely to read them and save them for future reference. As they are going to address a specific point, they allow you to be more relevant which, again, means more people read them.

Better still, as they start with a number and will be packed with key words, the search engines love them, which will generate even more added value… for you!

Relaunch your e-newsletter

The days of introspective newsletters promoting a new partner or a new office are over. People want to know what to do in certain situations so make full use of listicles and case studies so clients are getting that from your newsletter, not your competitors' one. If you are producing longer content, give them paragraph one and a link back to your site and the full article, rather than producing text-heavy pages.

Also, make sure your CRM system or marketing database can be split down so it only sends your content to those it is relevant to. This will immediately mark you out as a source or reference rather than an e-annoyance.

Use the news

The world is saturated by rolling news and popular culture. To bring your point to life, relate it to one of these sources – pick a heavily reported item and adapt it to make a point for the practice area you're promoting.

I have seen clients use a whole range of reference points, including highly charged incidents in the previous weekend's sports matches, celebrity chefs, high street retailers, and political leaders' faux pas. As long as it catches the eye, you can use it to make a legal point.

3. Openly promote 'five minutes'

I have no doubt at all that your fee earners are more than happy to give their clients and contacts five minutes on the phone to answer a quick question. The only thing is, do those clients know that facility is available to them? How well do you promote it?

To you, it's obvious, but make sure it's obvious to your clients. Then remind them. Then remind them again. The more frequently you can engage your fee earners and clients in conversation, the stronger your client relationships will be. And the more tangible benefit is, once they've got that first free bit of guidance, the chance of the instruction not coming to your firm is less than slim (which is something we'll look at in more detail in the next section of this chapter).

'Loss leaders' and how to use them

Loss leaders have been used by savvy marketers – particularly in the retail and FMCG sectors – for years. It is basically a term used to describe something you either give away free or at a fraction of its recommended retail price.

The idea is to persuade people to try you out so that you can either sell them more once you're in the door (supermarkets are the best exponents of that model) or so they come to trust you and increase the likelihood they'll buy more in the future (think of the little chunks of pie, cheese, or cake foisted on you as you walk around your local farmers' market).

In a legal context, loss leaders can be a good way to start to positively influence your targets' decision-making process. However, given you're paid ostensibly for your time, you have to make sure:

- What you are offering has minimal impact on your billable time; and
- Your efforts maximise the likelihood you will receive a volume of work sufficient to counterbalance your initial investment of time.

Loss leaders also have a close cousin in the 'negotiable variable', the little extras salesmen will throw into a deal to sweeten it and push it towards a close (think of the car dealer adding in a DAB radio or nice wheel trims to make sure you leave with the keys to a new car). This incarnation is arguably the one law firms can make better use of.

How could you use loss leaders in a legal context?

In simple terms, there are two different types of loss leaders a lawyer can offer:

1. The fixed free offer

This option is based on providing a piece of work on a fixed content/fixed outcome basis, and providing that work free of charge. For example, employment lawyers have long offered to review a clients' employment contracts, staff handbooks, or HR policies for free. The quid pro quo is that if (or when) those reviews uncover something of concern, the legal work required to rectify those concerns will go to the team who conducted the review.

Similarly, a private client practice might offer regular will reviews for their clients and, if situations have changed, they will outline possible changes the client may wish to make in order to protect their wealth and the future gains of their beneficiaries. Again, any additional work will go to the reviewer, which will more than cover the cost of the initial review. It could also uncover work for other professionals (tax accountants or financial advisers), which would provide invaluable referral opportunities that will generate their own financial wins for the reviewer under the laws of reciprocity.

Although these are two of the best known examples of loss leaders in a legal context, many firms are exploring more creative offerings, including reviews of website terms and conditions, business plan reviews, and feasibility studies relating to potential acquisitions. It's important to note that while I've described these as a 'free of charge' option, they can equally be charged for at a very low cost so that some of the time cost is recouped.

2. The initial free offer

This is where you would offer something free as a potential first step with the caveat that additional time and effort would be billed at your regular hourly rate. One of the most common examples of this option is the initial free consultation meeting offered by matrimonial lawyers who will explore the prospective client's circumstances and offer some initial suggestions as to the best way to proceed.

I have also worked with a charity team who offer a 'first question free' service whereby – you guessed it – a charity can ring up and ask a single question on any legal area for free. Not only does this allow them to stay in fairly regular contact with their clients, and with the charities in their local area they'd like to become their clients, it has also given them a concrete reason to go out to market which has boosted their profile within the charity sector and garnered them PR they probably would not have otherwise enjoyed.

How could you use negotiable variables in a legal context?

As I said a little earlier, a negotiable variable is a free extra you can include within a deal to make the deal sweeter for the client. It may be something you offer upfront as part of your initial pitch because experience has taught you similar clients have appreciated similar extras in the past. It may be something you keep up your sleeve until it comes to trying to close your prospect so you can inject the additional value required to push them over the line.

As I also said a little earlier, I think this is the option that can be used to best effect within the legal industry. Why? Because while these are free added extras (delivering the real added value we covered in the previous section of this chapter), they will sit alongside regular billable work, which means you are recovering your desired fee levels/hourly rate while you deliver these extras.

Another benefit of the negotiable variable is that it will help you stand out from any competitors in the picture. As you will, in the majority of cases at least, match each other's offers in terms of legal experience/technical delivery, you will be the one to stand up and say 'but what we will also do is factor in a few personalised extras that'll make sure you achieve the most effective way of working… for free'. This will immediately make your offering the most compelling and the most attractive.

So what types of things can you use as negotiable variables?
Some of the options I have seen used to good effect include:

- Tailoring bills to match the frequency and content the individual client prefers;
- Switching to electronic billing and/or acceptance into the client's electronic billing system;
- Assuming a non-exec position on the client's board to provide a legal perspective on all strategic decisions at source;
- A regular catch-up meeting to discuss possible opportunities and potential introductions for the client;
- Regular management training;
- Shared knowledge management resources;
- An email help desk to field simple questions as they arise;
- Hot-desking and mini-secondments;
- A range of automatic reviews of key contracts and supporting documents;
- The ability to use the law firm's meeting facilities; and
- Support (physical and financial) for the client's preferred charitable causes.

However, before you even make an offer or make a decision as to what to offer, do your preparation. The first rule is to identify and shortlist the types of things your prospect wants you to offer. This could be because you have worked with similar clients in the past (whether those similarities lie in the client's type, size, location, or personality) or (ideally) because you have also taken time during your initial conversations to actually ask and record what the prospect considers to be real added value.

If you go through this stage before you even attempt to use the negotiable variables at your disposal, you will automatically increase your chances of success because you will be offering what the clients want, and not what you think they should have. As with added value, too many firms still use what they have or have always done, rather than what a client actually wants, and are then surprised their approach hasn't worked despite having in their own minds – 'gone the extra mile'.

The other thing to bear in mind is if you don't have what you're being asked for, create it (as long as that is cost-effective of course), because the chances are a) if that client wants it, many others will too and b) if it is suggested by your target market, it could well be more relevant and innovative than any idea you (as a law firm) could come up with, which again will mark you out positively from your competition.

My last suggestion is make sure everything you come up with isn't kept as an internal secret. Be prepared to share your ideas with other departments, other offices, and other teams. All of your colleagues can make good use of your negotiable variables, and they may even be able to improve upon them using their own client experiences.

Make sure all of your fee earners not only understand your negotiable variables but also have the skills to utilise them in pitch situations, in tender documents, in more informal 'coffee' meetings, and in any other work-winning situation they regularly find themselves in. After all, if they can use your ideas to win more work, surely that benefits everyone, doesn't it?

Epilogue: **Is there actually a fifth 'P'?**

All the way back in Chapter 2, I introduced some principles I learned on the very first day of my marketing degree; namely, the 'marketing mix' and, more specifically, Dr Philip Kotler's four Ps:

1. **Product**: What do you offer your clients? How do you deliver those services? What is your client value proposition?
2. **Position**: How do you want to be perceived? Who are your competitors? Who do you want as your clients?
3. **Promotion**: How do you get what you have in front of the clients you want? What messages will you promote? What channels will you use to convey those messages most effectively?
4. **Price**: What level of pricing is congruent with your product and your (desired) market position? What fee levels would the clients you want expect? Where are the price sensitivities in your target markets?

From there, what I've endeavoured to do with this book is to explain how you can apply the four Ps to a 21st-century legal practice, so that the way you package, position, and promote your firm/department/practice will win not only more, but also better and more profitable new work.

To do that, we've worked through a very straightforward four-step process:

1. Building the right product;
2. Positioning that product at the right level of the legal market;
3. Promoting your offering to the right audience(s); and
4. Making sure you are priced correctly for your chosen audience.

Then we looked at some successful examples from the UK and US legal markets and I asked the people most heavily involved in the packaging and positioning of those initiatives how they had achieved what they wanted to achieve marketing-wise.

That, in a nutshell, is exactly what I wanted to achieve when I first set about writing this book. However, now that I'm sat here looking at the almost finished article, I can't help thinking that I missed a P – 'people'. If we look at the interviews in Chapter 6, people are central to everything the senior marketers and senior managers I spoke to have achieved.

John Seigal at Clintons placed enormous stock on recruiting the right people and keeping them in the firm. He also talked about having people with the right reputations and people willing to do the (subtle) activities that would allow them to sustain those reputations so that the best work always finds his firm.

Roger Inman at Stone King talked about building capacity and expertise in his team and filling any gaps by bringing in the right people from other firms. He talked about how he's built a team that has eight of the 27 top-ranked people in his sector. He also talked about finding ways for the people on both sides of the table (head teacher and lawyers) to work together more effectively so that the schools or trusts he was working with enjoyed the maximum benefit from Stone King's involvement.

Ian Turvill at Freeborn & Peters LLP talked about the fact that their sector choices had been made by the people they had in their partnership, and about how they had built their credibility through their CVs and then by adapting their marketing approach in each sector to the personal preferences of the people who made up their client base and target lists.

Jill Weber at Stinson Leonard Street talked about the need to upskill their attorneys via their proprietary 'Fast Forward' programme and although the primary effect of the programme was to increase revenues, it has also helped position the firm within the market as their client partners (as people) have got closer to their clients (as people). As a result, they are now thinking about their clients and the specific objectives of their businesses and are able to make the right introductions and provide the right information to help those clients achieve those objectives.

Angela Hickey at Levenfeld Pearlstein talked about embedding the 'LP Way' into the minds of the people at every level of their firm. The LP Way was built as a means of establishing an exceptional level of client experience for the people the firm worked with. It was made possible inside the firm by the firm's leadership, and the fact they were so long-serving and well established, as well as the people throughout the firm who bought into the LP Way.

Karl Chapman at Riverview Law talked about bringing the right people with the right values into his organisation and building teams that included a variety of people with very different but complementary skills, i.e. the solicitors, project managers, techies, and client managers, so that his clients get the highest levels of service and the highest levels of value from instructing Riverview.

To me, the reason all of these examples were a success came down to the people involved; people are completely integral to the success of the four Ps.

1. Product

You need the right people to deliver your product, and they need to deliver it in the right way. Your people also need to be the living embodiment of your client value proposition if it is going to take root and appear credible.

You also need a product that serves the people you want as clients in the way they want to be served. The only way you can achieve that is to recruit the right people and train them in the right way; and to talk to the people who buy your services so you can continually refine your coverage, quality, and delivery so that you remain the most attractive option to your clients, contacts, and targets.

2. Position

Once you know the people who use your firm and the people you want to use your firm, you can position yourself according to their requirements, preferences, and perceptions. You can create a personality – a brand even – that will resonate with those people and make it obvious that you are the type of firm they want to work with. However, in order to find all of that out – and market test it to make sure your position is attainable and sustainable – you will need to get your people to engage with the people in your market(s) and ensure you are what you need to be as far as those markets are concerned.

You also need to make sure your people are ready to service the level of the market you have positioned yourself within, in a way that is congruent with your market position. If you are a high-end, service-led private client practice, your people have to provide the level of service that client base expects as standard, consistently and across the board. If you have positioned yourself as hugely attentive and as a group of individuals who pride themselves on attention to detail, your people can't afford to come late to a meeting, misread the date in an email, or sit playing with their phones during client meetings, even if they're only one of a team who attends.

3. Promotion

This is probably the easiest P to tie down to people. If your promotional activity is going to work, it needs to speak directly to your clients and to the people you want to be your clients. Make sure your message is one that will be attractive to and understood by the people you are trying to influence, and make sure it is being delivered via the channels that those people actually use.

Again, to answer those questions your people need to be talking to your clients and to the people within your target markets to find out how well your promotional activity is working and to make sure your promotion is keeping you visible to the people within your market(s).

4. Price

From an internal perspective, pricing has of course to be set according to the number and level of people that will be involved in delivering the work. However, if you really want to use pricing to your advantage marketing-wise, you need to go out and discuss the different pricing options you should be offering with your clients. Do they want fixed fees? Do they want to explore risk-reward type structures? Most importantly, you need to ensure your clients are prepared to bear your fee levels – or are you out of kilter (and that means higher or lower) with the other firms that make up your chosen level within the legal market?

From an administrative point of view, you need to discuss the frequency and transparency of your billing. Could you provide more detail more often, or are you producing an Amazonian rainforest-threatening amount of paper bills when a more infrequent electronic billing mechanism may be more attractive to your clients?

Similarly, you need to stay up to date with what your clients consider to be real added value and where you can strengthen your service offering, which in turn will strengthen your current client and referrer relationships and make you more attractive to the people you want to be your new clients or new referrers.

All those questions can only be answered if your people are talking to your clients.

Now, I'm not going to renege on the basic premise of the book; in order to survive in an increasingly competitive and complicated market, and faced with an increasingly demanding and fickle consumer, law firms will most definitely need to package and position themselves in a more sophisticated way. If firms are going to stand out in an increasingly crowded market, they simply have to formulate a stronger client value proposition and promote that proposition more effectively through the channels most likely to place it in front of the right people.

It's worth noting, though, that however clever you are with your packaging, positioning, proposition, and promotion, none of this will work without people:

- You need the right people internally, and those people need to buy in totally to what you are trying to do and know exactly what part you expect them to play in the implementation of your ideas;
- You need to be mindful of the 'people factor' when you examine the culture of your firm (whether that's the culture you have or the culture you want) and when you come to decide what you need to do to make sure your people display the right values and behaviours and effect the right actions so you achieve your desired market position;
- You need to keep developing your people so they have the required skills and, if necessary, top up their enthusiasm and hone their focus to ensure a consistency of performance – you'll also need to invest in client research and speak to the people who buy your services to make sure your efforts are working;
- You also need to stay mindful that your clients are people too. You need to create proper working relationships and establish an effective, open dialogue, with them;

- You need to actively manage those relationships (and review them regularly to make sure any potential issues are resolved quickly), and keep adding value to those relationships wherever you can; and
- Looking at the 'people factor' in a wider perspective, if you are considering merging you will need to consider the 'softer' side: do your values, culture, and people complement those of the firm you'd like to merge with? Your new firm's success is dependent on seamless integration, and if your people, values, and culture don't match, that is highly unlikely to happen.

Yes, in order to profit you do need to package and position your firm correctly, but if the 'people' element isn't addressed, you could very well be setting all your good work up to fail.

www.ingramcontent.com/pod-product-compliance
Ingram Content Group UK Ltd.
Pitfield, Milton Keynes, MK11 3LW, UK
UKHW021846150926
8657IPUK00005B/95

9 781783 582822